time of utter despair. With the help of stirring anecdotes about their son, family and religion, Sherri Mandell has told a beautiful story of a horrendous crime that defies any sense of logic or rationale."

GARY ROSENBLATT, *The Jewish Week*
"I was, admittedly, less than anxious to read Sherri Mandell's *The Blessing of a Broken Heart*, knowing it would tell a tragic story of unending pain. And it does. But somehow, this chronicle of a mother dealing with the brutal murder of her 13-year-old son, Koby, passes through to the other side of tragedy, offering an inspiring reflection on the life lessons learned from a senseless death....Hers is the wisdom gained from coming to terms with, and accepting, tragedy, and she shares it generously with us."

YOSSI KLEIN HALEVI, Israel correspondent, *The New Republic*
"With remarkable self-awareness, Sherri Mandell guides us through the abyss, and shows the way out. She describes the precise point where the human ability to cope falters and the wisdom of the soul prevails. There is great strength here—in the observations of her own grieving and healing process, in the writing and most of all in her surprisingly deepening faith. Like Mandell, you will emerge from this encounter broken and more whole. An urgent, devastating and yes, wonderful, book."

MICHAEL B. OREN, Author, *Six Days of War*
"Powerful and impassioned, uplifting and devastating both, Sherri Mandell's breathtaking prose takes the reader to the depths of pain and to faith's pinnacle. *The Blessing of a Broken Heart* is the ultimate testament of a woman's love for her son, for her country, and for God. Readers will never forget it."

Sherri Mandell

The
BLESSING
of a
BROKEN
HEART

The Toby Press

The Toby Press

Second Edition 2003

The Toby Press LLC
POB 8531, New Milford, CT. 06676-8531, USA
& POB 2455, London W1A 5WY, England
www.tobypress.com

The right of Sherri Mandell to be identified as the author
of this work has been asserted by her in accordance with the
Copyright, Designs & Patents Act 1988

Back cover photograph © Nancy Lederman

ISBN 1 59264 029 X, *hardcover*

A CIP catalogue record for this title is available
from the British Library

Typeset in Garamond by Jerusalem Typesetting

Printed and bound in the United States by
Thomson-Shore Inc., Michigan

In loving memory of

Yaakov Natan Mandell
(June 14, 1987–May 8, 2001)

and

Yosef Ish-Ran
(January 3, 1987–May 8, 2001)

Koby   *Yosef*

Contents

PART ONE: THE CAVE, 1

Chapter one: The Cave, 3

Chapter two: The Vessel, 5

Chapter three: The New Land, 9

Chapter four: Contractions of Death, 13

Chapter five: Koby's Death, 17

Chapter six: The Messiah and the
Day that Koby was Born, 25

Chapter seven: Elijah's Appearance at
Koby's Circumcision, 31

Chapter eight: The World-to-Come, 41

Chapter nine: Potato Chips at the Funeral, 45

Chapter ten: The Shiva and the Faces of God, 51

Chapter eleven: The Canyon and the Spring, 57

Chapter twelve: Entering the Sabbath, *65*

Chapter thirteen: Levels of Pain, *71*

Chapter fourteen: The Bullet and the Jewelry Box, *73*

Chapter fifteen: The Shooting Star, *81*

Chapter sixteen: Koby's Birthday—
Becoming Holy Beggars, *85*

Chapter seventeen: The Bar Mitzvah, *89*

Chapter eighteen: The Cricket, *93*

Chapter nineteen: The Broken Glass, *97*

Chapter twenty: Shimon Bar Yochai, *99*

Chapter twenty-one: Guilt, *105*

PART TWO: THE BIRD'S NEST, 109

Chapter twenty-two: Hope, *111*

Chapter twenty-three: Bird Stories, *115*

Chapter twenty-four: Thanksgiving Blessings, *123*

Chapter twenty-five: First Born, *127*

Chapter twenty-six: Chanukah, *133*

Chapter twenty-seven: Faith, *137*

Chapter twenty-eight: The Language of God, *143*

Chapter twenty-nine: Signs and Dreams, *147*

Chapter thirty: The Family, *151*

Chapter thirty-one: The Reporters, *155*

Chapter thirty-two: Pain and Forgiveness, *159*

Chapter thirty-three: God's Silence, *161*

Chapter thirty-four: A Hierarchy of Suffering, *165*

Chapter thirty-five: Purim, *167*

Chapter thirty-six: My Grandmother's Mantra, *173*

Chapter thirty-seven: Humility, *177*

Chapter thirty-eight: Heaven, *181*

Chapter thirty-nine: The Deer, *183*

Chapter forty: Our Wedding Anniversary, *187*

Chapter forty-one: Not Knowing, *191*

Chapter forty-two: Passover 2002, *193*

Chapter forty-three: Jacob's Ladder, *197*

Chapter forty-four: Another Shimon
Bar Yochai Story, *201*

Chapter forty-five: The Koby Mandell Foundation, *203*

Chapter forty-six: Gulls on the Beach, *207*

Chapter forty-seven: The Bird's Nest, *211*

Chapter forty-eight: A Year On, *219*

Chapter forty-nine: Koby's Articles, *223*

Appendix: About the Foundation, *227*

Bibliography, 229

Acknowledgments, 231

"I needed to learn everything I could about the soul. He was in a different land now. If he'd gone to China, I'd want to know about China. I wanted to know where he was."

Sharon Weinstock, mother of Yitzhak,
killed in 1993 in a terrorist attack in Israel.

"Who prepares nourishment for the raven, when its children cry out to God, confused without food?"

Job, Chapter 38, verse 41

Part one:
The Cave

Chapter one
The Cave

The cave is in the canyon half a mile from my home in Tekoa. Thousands of years of rainwater have carved this opening in the limestone. Facing the Dead Sea with its back to Jerusalem, twelve miles away, the cave can only be reached by a steep climb down craggy paths that shepherds wander, weeds and wild flowers choking the landscape. It is easy to stumble on the sharp stones that jut from the ground. Two thousand years ago, those fleeing for their lives hid here; later, in the fifth century, others chose to live in the wadi for the solitude. Monks hollowed some of these caves and studied and prayed here. But most of the caves are uninhabitable. There is one cave that I am most afraid of—the cave where my son spent his last hours.

A cave is a place of constriction, of darkness, of fear. It is like the darkness from before light was created. The cave is moist, slippery; a hollow that reverberates with secrets and all that has been lost. Moses and Shimon Bar Yochai and Eliyahu all dwelled in caves, and encountered God from the clefts in the rock. They each entered the cramped space of fear, pain, and darkness—in order to find the truths they were seeking.

My thirteen-year-old son Koby entered the cave—but he did not emerge. I thought my family and I would be lost in a cave of grief, forever wandering in a labyrinth so dark you can't even see your own hand, but have to trust that when you step, the ground will still be under you.

Chapter two

The Vessel

Koby was my first child, the child who taught me to be a mother. I had three kids in three years, one four years later, and Koby often helped me keep my sense of humor when taking care of children became difficult. Once, when Koby was four, I served soup, and Koby spilled the soup all over the table and floor; then just as I cleaned all that up, Daniel spilled the soup, and when I cleaned that up, Eliana's soup spilled. I started screaming in frustration and was about to totally lose it, when Koby said to me: "Don't worry Mom, it's only chicken soup." He was right. He calmed me down by saying that. He had a way of putting things in perspective.

I could have stayed in bed the rest of my life mourning him. I could have remained broken, resenting my life, my lot. But there is something in me that refuses to be broken, no matter how intense the pain, something that moves toward the light.

This wholeness was demonstrated to me recently when we were on an archaeological dig with ten other bereaved families. We have created a foundation in Koby's memory, the Koby Mandell Foundation, and we run a camp and healing retreats in Israel for family members of victims of terror. Our intention for the dig was to bring families together to enjoy an activity that at the same time might also act as a metaphor and embody what the entire family sometimes needs to do with grief—plunge into it, together, each in their own way.

We were at the archeological site of Beit Guvrin, not far from the city of Kiryat Gat. Caves scattered throughout the site house ancient olive presses and other artifacts. Our group walked through the rain to a cave and climbed down into the darkness, the kids running, the parents stepping gingerly. We began to dig through the ruins. Over two thousand years ago, when the Hasmoneans conquered, the Edomites were forced to convert or leave. Those who fled left their belongings behind.

The guide explained that we were in the basement of one of the houses that had been abandoned. We took shovels and began plunging in the ground, and then sifting through the buckets of dirt, discovering shards of pottery identifiable as broken handles of cups or bases of vases. We dug for a few hours, the children and the parents all together. And then suddenly, somebody unearthed an entire vessel, about the size of a jug of wine, made of clay, the entire pot intact, whole.

After all the time that had elapsed, all the generations that had died and been born, something whole remained. And the same is true for those of us who feel the suffering of loss. There is something in us that clings to life and refuses to be diminished or broken. We ourselves are vessels, filled with Godliness. And though we may chip and crack, our souls are whole even when we aren't.

I have not come to this belief in the soul easily. Often my belief flies away. But that is the nature of my faith. When God created heaven and earth, the Bible states 'the spirit of God hovered over the face of the water.' Rashi* compares the spirit of God to a dove hovering over its nest. God's presence is like that too: it does not usually force you to recognize it, but is something that covers

---

* Rabbi Solomon Ben Isaac, the foremost Biblical commentator, who lived in the 12th century in France.

you, and then alights; something that doesn't stay put, but flies off just when you may be looking for it.

Since Koby's death, the spirit of God has hovered over me, flickering and returning. There have been moments of revelation, moments when I felt that God was touching me, pointing me, moving me, hugging me. They are inner moments, windows that open so that I can view my son's death in a different light.

Sometimes I feel as if I'm trying to weave all this loss into something beautiful. To make his absence a presence. The web is fragile and can be broken with a child's pinky. I know that. Still, I feel it is my job to keep weaving Koby's strength and beauty into the world.

I know that my broken heart will never be the same. I will always long for Koby and feel the pain of his absence. But it is possible to build a new heart. Last summer, after going to the camp with other children who lost siblings or parents to terror, my daughter Eliana explained to me why she liked the camp so much: "It's like we touched each others hearts," she said. "We put our hearts together, and we made a new heart." That's what I hope this book will do for you, because many of us live with broken hearts. But when you touch broken hearts together, a new heart emerges, one that is more open and compassionate, able to touch others, a heart that seeks God. That is the blessing of a broken heart.

Chapter three

The New Land

Koby did not intend to die a martyr. What he intended was to cut school with his friend Yosef—the two of them innocent as Tom Sawyer. Mark Twain writes: "Tom did play hooky, and he had a very good time." Koby and Yosef were also looking for a good time. Instead, they were killed.

A thirteen and a fourteen-year-old boy hiking into a canyon one hundred yards from our home in Tekoa, treading a path that threads its way to the Dead Sea, ten miles away. Sometimes, if the weather is crisp and clear or there's been a rainfall, you can look out over the Judean Hills and see the tongue of the Dead Sea, gray-blue, visible through a cleft in the mountain. If you didn't know, you'd think it was a cloud. Instead, it's a glimpse of the lowest point on earth.

My view has been irreparably changed, damaged. Yet I like to think that Koby is still in my view, invisible for the time being. I have a feeling that one day, the veil separating us will disappear, the clouds will part, and there he will be—strong, brave, and handsome. I will instantly recognize him by the sound of his voice, his smell, and the power of his hug.

I have a feeling that though I can't see him, he is hovering over me, like the butterflies in the canyon. The week before the murder, my neighbor Zvi, a computer expert from California, told me he'd been hiking in the canyon and flocks of white butterflies fluttered overhead as he walked with his son. The morning of the murder Zvi and his son were also down in the canyon, a different part, about an eighth of a mile from the boys. Zvi and his son heard nothing except the silence.

Though Zvi didn't hear my son's murder, my son's death did not go unnoticed. About the time of the murder, a deer charged out of the wadi and stole into our village, into the yard of a woman named Zahava, who works in the local nursery school. The deer stepped right up to her window. His coat was muddy, his legs covered in blood. Afraid, she threw a stone at him but he wouldn't move. She didn't understand why he wouldn't leave her yard.

I think he wouldn't go back because he was scared. He had seen the horror that had been inflicted on two innocent children. He was frightened to return to the canyon, the dry riverbed, to his home. He knew that a place that was once pure had been forever stained with the evil human beings can inflict when they are committed to hate.

Hate can steal a person's soul. But I will not let it. Instead, I will learn about the soul, about the new land Koby and I share. I will learn the customs and the language, to translate the signs I might otherwise miss; how to receive the divine messages I have been sent: messages about Elijah, Shimon Bar Yochai, and the Messiah; birds, angels, and the jewel of the soul. My life feels like a spiritual mystery, with symbols that beg to be decoded. Since Koby's death, I have had moments of peering through the curtain of ordinary reality, touching something greater, deeper, more extraordinary. Sometimes I think that God and Koby are in cahoots, preparing these moments for me. I pray to my son, and I can't help but feel that Koby sends me his blessing. And I hope that through telling my story, you, the reader will be blessed, better able to recognize the blessings in your own pain and struggle to lead a life of meaning.

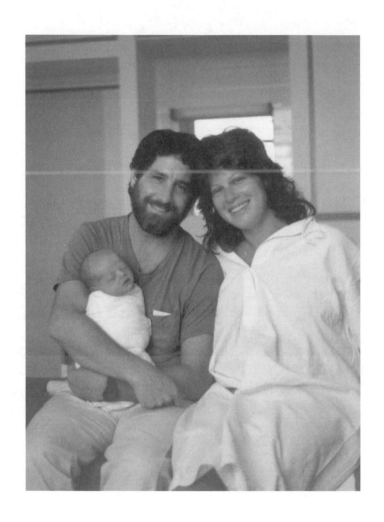

Chapter four

Contractions of Death

Mourning my son has similarities to labor. The contractions of pain rush through my body like a knot that is tied tighter and tighter so that I am unable to breathe, dead along with my son. My womb becomes a grave. I feel the pain of him in my belly, a pressure bearing down on me. It will always be inside of me. And though I hope and pray that one day I will not be as great with pain as I am now, the pain will never leave me.

Still, it feels like I am pregnant, pregnant with death, giving birth to a new self—a self that can navigate the depths of suffering and yet go on with life. A self that can live in two worlds, this world and the world of the soul. Because I know I must find a way to reach the eternity within me so that I can meet him where he is.

I try to remember my son's face. It is difficult for me to picture him clearly in my mind, to retrieve his physical presence. I will no longer gaze at his beautiful face, admiring his almost-man's contours with the eyebrows that were beginning to fill in, becoming more feathered at the inside edge. I took pleasure in his growth, admired his ever increasing height. I enjoyed his first sprinklings of pimples, the smell of him as he became a man. I felt that as he grew, I grew. As he grew, I too was bigger, stronger, more powerful.

Just the night before he died, he lifted me up in his arms, showing me how strong he was. Then we measured and compared ourselves in the mirror, standing back to back. He was a fraction of an inch shorter than me. And now he will never reach me. I am left to do the growing for both of us.

I remember his birth, the joy of being pregnant. In 1987, when I was pregnant with Koby, I felt like I was walking around with a special secret. I wondered why nobody had told me how precious I would feel carrying a baby in my belly. It was like there was a jewel inside of me, shimmering and beautiful and full of lights and colors.

A few weeks before Koby was born, I had a dream where I was in a hospital bed. I'd just given birth and was filling out a form which had one question: condition of mother at birth. I wrote: Bliss.

And when he was born, after thirteen hours of labor, that is exactly how I felt, holding him to me. Bliss.

Even though Koby was blue and had to be slapped so that his breathing started, I hardly worried. I recognized him immediately as mine, as a soul that was connected to me. He looked just like my father's family, a little old man, the grandfather I'd never seen. He looked like he was all soul and had traveled to us from a distant land to which he was still clinging.

Now, my beloved son, you have returned to a distant land and bliss is a word that has been erased from my life. Yet I believe you are in bliss. You became part of Jewish history, dead because you were in an isolated place where Palestinians steeped in hatred found an opportunity to give vent to it.

Jewish tradition tells us that when a righteous person's soul returns to God, the soul is in a state of bliss, reuniting with God. I imagine God's joy in seeing you, in meeting your sparkling intelligence, your lack of artifice, your basic goodness.

I imagine you, the family historian, recounting the days of our years. I imagine you pleading with God to bestow blessing on your family.

14

When you died, part of me died too. I couldn't eat anything for three days. My friends begged me to eat something. Finally, I said: "I'll eat watermelon." I didn't remember that I had eaten watermelon at your birth. But as I ate it, I remembered being in the hospital room with you the day after your birth. I nursed you and held you to me, and then ate the watermelon my friend Ella had brought me. As the sun rose and the birds called out to me, a chorus of cheeps and squawks, you and I nestled together like a mother bird in her nest with her baby bird, and I felt that the whole world was nursing or suckling.

Now, after your death, the watermelon reminds me of fertility, a pregnant belly, the rosy flush of creation. But a circle has closed. I eat watermelon again. It feels as if I am giving birth to your soul, a soul free of the constraints of body, a soul that can fly up to God and bask in delights. I am giving birth to the new purpose in my life—to live with an awareness of the soul, to recognize God's hand in my life. It is a labor fraught with pain, a labor that will continue for months, for years—maybe for a lifetime.

The pain is a cave in which you can lose your path and never find the opening. The pain is quicksand; in a minute you can drown. The morning after the funeral, my head was pounding. I lay in bed, crying, and my friend Leah, a nurse, came up the stairs. She said: "Here take this," and tried to hand me a valium. "No," I said. "I gave birth without drugs and I'll do this without drugs."

I want to feel the pain—for if I go into my pain and truly experience it, swim in it, there is a chance I will emerge on the other shore of my loss, still pained and struggling, but with a different vision. And if I don't, I will always be living in the land of suffering. One who enters this pain understands that death is part of life, and is here, always. Death now is something that will release me and allow me to see Koby again. Death no longer scares me.

2 Jewish Teenagers Are Beaten to Death in the West Bank

By JOEL GREENBERG

TEKOA, West Bank, May 9 — Two schoolboys from this Jewish settlement who skipped class to go hiking in a nearby gorge were found bludgeoned to death in a cave today, and the police said they were killed by Palestinians.

Prime Minister Ariel Sharon expressed "deep shock" at the deaths and called them an escalation of Palestinian terrorism against innocent civilians. He accused the Palestinian Authority of failing to stop the violence and of inciting murder in its official news media.

A police spokesman said that the two boys, Yaakov Mandel, 13, and Yosef Ishran, 14, had been battered to death with rocks. "Their heads were crushed," he said. The blood-stained rocks were found near the bodies in Wadi Haritun, a dry riverbed near Tekoa in the Judean Desert south of Bethlehem. The police said that they believed the two boys had died in an apparent chance encounter with their attackers.

The deaths came two days after a 4-month-old Palestinian baby girl was killed by Israeli tank fire and further roiled emotions in a week of spiraling violence that neither side seems able to control.

After the bodies were found, more than a dozen Palestinians were rounded up for questioning from the neighboring village of Tukua, and the road to the village was blocked with a trench. Defense Minister Binyamin Ben-Eliezer promised to track down those responsible for the deaths, "one by one."

Saeb Erakat, a member of the Palestinian cabinet, said, "The Palestinian Authority regrets the loss of life of these two boys and all children, be it Israeli or Palestinian, Jewish, Muslim or Christian."

He said that "killing civilians is a crime whether on the Palestinian or the Israeli side."

But Yasir Arafat, the Palestinian leader, avoided a direct response to a reporter's question about the killing of the Israeli boys, saying that a Palestinian baby who was wounded in fighting today "was exposed to the same tragedy."

He was referring to new fighting that broke out in the Gaza Strip where the baby and her mother were wounded by Israeli fire in Rafah. Elsewhere in the Gaza Strip today, Israeli troops twice entered Palestinian-controlled territory near Beit Hanun, uprooting orchards and demolishing a Palestinian police post after mortars were fired into Israel. The mortars landed near Kibbutz Kfar Aza, but no one was killed.

The family of one of the teenage victims, Yaakov Mandel, moved to Israel five years ago from Silver Spring, Md., and he held both American and Israeli citizenship, friends

Rina Castelnuovo for The New York Times

Sheri and Seth Mandel cry over the body of their 13-year-old son Yaakov, who, along with 14-year-old Yosef Ishran, was found bludgeoned to death in a cave in the Judean Desert near their West Bank settlement home.

The New York Times

Two Jewish schoolboys were found dead in a cave near Tekoa.

said. His aunt, Loren Fogelson, of Nassau County, said in a telephone interview today: "He was a warm, loving, peace-loving, caring boy, the kind of son that every mother would love to have. Our hearts are broken. It's a nightmare."

The American ambassador to Israel, Martin Indyk, said the United States was outraged by the "vicious murder."

The teenagers' bodies were discovered by search parties before dawn today after the boys failed to return home on Tuesday night. They skipped school and went hiking with-

The Israeli police blame Palestinians, who cite a cycle of killings of civilians.

out telling their parents, who thought they had gone after classes to a demonstration in Jerusalem, where settlers protested what they said was the government's failure to ensure their security. When the boys failed to return by midnight, the parents alerted the security forces.

The boys went to hike in Wadi Haritun, a scenic gorge flanked by steep cliffs and caves that is only a 15-minute walk from Tekoa.

Teenagers from the settlement said that they regularly went there for hikes and bonfires, even during the recent months of Palestinian unrest, often without the armed escort that isrequired by the army. "It's our backyard," said Aviva Sutnick, 15. "We don't have too many places here for teenagers to hang out."

Palestinian shepherds and people from neighboring Arab villages also visit the gorge, but settlers said no violence had occurred there during the recent months of Israeli-Palestinian fighting.

Settlers reported that 100 goats

were stolen on Tuesday night from Tekoa, but the police said they did not know whether the theft was related to the killings.

Shaul Goldstein, the head of the local settler's council, warned that the continuing deadly Palestinian attacks could push some settlers to seek revenge. Settlers have been a main target of the seven-month-old Palestinian uprising, and dozens have been killed or wounded, many in drive-by shootings on West Bank roads.

"If the government and the army do not respond appropriately to this criminal incident, I'm afraid that the short fuse of the settlers and the anger that has accumulated in the last seven months could ignite in an uncontrolled way," Mr. Goldstein said.

At the funeral for the two boys, Rabbi Shlomo Riskin of the neighboring settlement of Efrat called for divine vengeance against "this cruel enemy that deliberately murders innocent children."

In her remarks, Education Minister Limor Livnat called the killings "a moral stain on the Palestinian people that will never be erased."

"This is our country, we've come home and we're here to stay," Mrs. Livnat asserted. "The murderers will not stay, because we are stronger than them. With God's help, we shall win."

Chapter five

Koby's Death

Koby's death is a Biblical death. It is a murder that is shocking in its raw pain, its unmediated cruelty. Two Jewish boys, my son, Koby Mandell, and his friend, Yosef Ish-Ran were attacked in a cave by Arab terrorists, and bludgeoned to death with stones the size of bowling balls. I can't think about a murderer pummeling my child to death with rocks. I don't know how to cope with the pain and the evil. I imagine my son afraid, crying out, dying alone, in horror and agony. A thirteen-year-old boy.

Anachronistic, primitive in its horror, the murder hearkens back to the first murder in the world. In his jealousy, Cain slew his brother Abel with stones, and the Bible tells us that "his blood cried out from the ground." The boys' blood was wiped all over the cave. The murderers have not been caught.

On the High Holy days, *Rosh HaShana* and *Yom Kippur*, in the prayer *Unetaneh Tokef*, we recite that God decides on this day: "who shall live and who shall die; who by fire, and who by water, who by sword, and who by wild beast; who by famine, and who by thirst, who by strangling, and who by stoning." David Wolpe in *Making*

Loss Matter says in regard to the prayer that "the words are specific and tied to the medieval age in which they were written." He says that the modern day equivalent is death by AIDS and cancer, or by car accidents.

But my son died in a barbaric murder, and blatant, overpowering hate was the agent of his death. How could God decide to kill the boys in such a cruel way? How can we live with such a gruesome death?

Since Koby's murder, I am unable to read the paper or listen to the news because what I hear is pain. The television broadcast on NBC, CNN, the articles in the *Jerusalem Report*, the *New York Times*, the *Washington Post*, *Newsday*... none of them got it right. They wanted sound bites, fast information. They wanted to sell newspapers with our tragedy.

The story was reported around the world in every major newspaper. Each article had a mistake or two—and they said nothing about what was important to us: the way that you had left the house that morning, laughing and happy; the fear when we waited for your return; the way my friend Shira told me that you were dead, intercepting the police, she told me later, so that she could tell me with love.

When I watch the attack on the World Trade Center, all I think about are the mothers. I feel like a voyeur and can no longer listen. Because I know that behind the news are families that are suffering. And I know that suffering is a knife that keeps digging into the most tender areas, and then pierces even deeper.

At 7:00 A.M. on May 8, 2001, I listened to the radio as I made Koby two salami sandwiches. I went up to get dressed and came downstairs. Yosef came to pick him up at 7:20 A.M. and I thought good, maybe Koby will get to school on time today. I didn't kiss him goodbye because Yosef was there so I just went upstairs to finish getting ready. That was the last time I saw my son.

At 8:00 A.M., I left to go swimming about twenty minutes away with a friend. Then I hitched about thirty minutes into Jerusalem for three meetings. I got to town a little early so I sat and drank coffee and edited a manuscript for my friend, Arieh—a murder mystery. I had edited up to page 25, but had grabbed the wrong pages that morning and had taken pages 106–126 by mistake. I began to edit them, when suddenly I was in the murder scene. A star basketball player gets murdered, pummeled in the head with a baseball bat. As I edited, I thought: What does Arieh know about murder? What do I know about murder? How can I edit a murder scene? Later I had a meeting with the editor of *Hadassah* magazine, where we discussed article assignments for the coming year. Mine was to write an article on miracles.

My husband, Seth, then a freelance business writer, was in Tekoa, working at home, so I didn't worry much about the kids. I called at three o'clock and got no answer. I called again at four o'clock and spoke to my husband, who told me that all the kids were out. In Tekoa, it's common for the kids to be out all day. They come home from school, throw down their bags, and go right back out, to the basketball court, or to friends, or to afternoon activities. So I wasn't worried.

I got home a little before 6:00 P.M. and asked my husband: "Where's Koby?" My middle son, Daniel, then eleven years old, wasn't home either but on an overnight school trip. We heard the six o'clock news, which reported that a child had been killed on a school trip, hit by a falling branch near the Jordan River. My husband immediately got on the Internet to check the news and make sure that Daniel was safe.

Then, at about 8:30 P.M., my ten-year-old daughter, Eliana, returned from youth group activities. I hoped that she had seen Koby but she told me that she hadn't seen him. I put the two smaller children to sleep and then I began to really worry.

I call Koby's friends and Yosef's mother, Rena. She says that she thinks they might have gone to the demonstration in Jerusalem calling for more protection for our roads and settlements. Another mother tells me that the road from Jerusalem to Tekoa is closed. It's often closed because of shootings from Beit Jalla. So I think to myself: it will take him a while to get home, but he'll get home. Then at ten o'clock at night I begin to dial madly. I call Koby's friends in Efrat and Jerusalem. I call Rena four times, who assures me that they're at the demonstration. Rena's husband is an Israeli policeman so I take comfort in the thought that she would know if they were in danger. She says they're on their way home, not to worry. Then, suddenly, it's eleven o'clock and Koby isn't home. I call the police. They check the hitchhiking posts.

My neighbor, Orly, who is a sabra, a native Israeli, comes over and calls Koby's teacher and is told: he hasn't been in school. Neither has Yosef. I still don't panic. I think: he's with Yosef. Something must have happened but they'll be home soon. Then Shlomo, Koby's friend, comes over and tells us that Koby and Yosef had said they were going to the wadi—a dry riverbed that cuts through a magnificent rugged canyon nearby. They must have gotten lost, I think. The Haritun Cave in Tekoa (named after Hartiun, a fifth century monk who established both a monastery and study cells in the wadi) is among the largest in the Middle East, with sixty chambers that extend two miles. He's stuck somewhere in there: it's happened to other kids before. He'll come home and I'll yell at him, and we'll go on. I truly think I'll suffer nothing more than lost sleep.

All night there are neighbors in my house. They say: "Welcome to the teen years. He's your oldest. We've all been through this."

I believe them. I can't accept that Koby isn't safe. I can't allow myself to think that something has happened to him.

But Koby has never done anything like this before. No matter what, he doesn't worry me. Because if there is one thing I am sure of, it is his love. He would worry me a little, but not like this.

The other mothers sit in my house, reassuring me. He's the oldest, this is your initiation, they do foolish things. They worry us. One's fourteen-year-old daughter had been missing until three o'clock one morning. One's eight-year-old son had been lost in the cave. Two ten-year-olds had taken the bus to Kiryat Shmona, a four hour trip, without telling anybody. "We think they're like us, but they're not. They have their own logic, their own way. They don't think like we do," Orly tells me.

Then the policemen march in, rifles slung over their shoulders, with beautiful and young faces, asking questions, filling out their papers. 'Go find them,' I want to shout, 'just go find them.' But I answer their questions.

I ask Orly for a glass of wine. I think: he's on his way home. Just be calm. It's all going to be okay.

Search crews from the area scour the wadi. They will find them, I think. They are lost, stuck, waiting. Pini Birnbaum, a twenty-three-year-old with American parents, who grew up here and knows the caves inside out, returns after three hours. He's been calling and shouting, but there has been no answer. "Since the caves are so big, there's still a chance they're in there," he tells us. That is the hope I cling to. I imagine them, stuck on some ledge in the cave, unable to go up or down, to rise or fall. Or they are on a bus to Eilat—on a whim—they aren't in the wadi at all, they've decided to get away from the madness here. It's a foolish act, but it makes sense: they are living in a war zone. They've been through eight months of the Intifada—of drive-by shootings every day. People could crack and just run away. Could do things that weren't like them. They could.

Shoshana sits knitting in my living room. She has three boys in the army. She says: "Go see if you can feel him somewhere, feel his being."

It's already four o'clock in the morning. Seth and I go out looking for him. We walk to the entrance of the wadi, less than five minutes away. I don't feel him. We see a van with two security men inside. They say they've searched all over. A crew of searchers will continue when the sun comes up. My legs begin to buckle, but I'm sure he'll come home. But when the sun rises and they're still not home, it hits me. They need to come home now. I remember something about missing children—if they aren't found the first day, chances are they won't be found alive. I plead with God and with Koby: Come back now! Come back now! I remember giving birth and how the midwife, worried after listening to Koby's heartbeat, said: push this baby out! push this baby out! I say: Come home now! come home now! with the same kind of urgency. I can will him to come home. I pace in front of the house. At 6:00 A.M., my husband walks to the synagogue, hoping that the strength of his prayers will bring the boys home.

In the house, my friends sit around me. I say: "He's okay, right, he's okay?" My friend Shira walks into the house and I see the fire of fear in her eyes and I know that there's pain there, more pain than I am willing to admit, to let enter my heart. Now I know that I am being too optimistic.

I say: "I'm going in the backyard." I think I can protect myself, as if bad news can only come to the front door. Then Shira comes out to me a short while later. She looks at me, takes my hand in hers, and says: "They found them. They're dead."

I say: "No he's not. Koby is not dead. He's not dead. He's not dead."

There is one thing I know: I do not want to live in a world where Koby is dead. Even worse, where Koby is murdered.

Friends tell me I fainted. I remember lying on the dirt in my backyard. Just lying there. I remember holding my husband, holding him and crying. I remember people talking to us about telling the other kids. Seth went up to tell them.

The two little ones were asleep. Seth woke Eliana, ten, and told her. She said: "Stop joking Daddy."

Gavi, six, just listened. And then they both curled up and went back to sleep.

They told Daniel on the school trip. The kids had heard on the radio that two boys from Tekoa were missing. Daniel had a feeling it was Koby, because Koby had been talking to him about wanting to go to the wadi. Then later, the person in charge of the trip took Daniel off the bus and told him that his brother was dead. The whole class got back on the bus and drove home. Daniel sobbed all three hours and then my whole village could hear him crying as he returned from the trip and ran to the house. I held him and held him and his crying was raspy and it was hard for him to breathe. He cried as if he was crying for all the pain in the world that was, and would ever be.

22

Now I am like the canary in the mine. I have been sent out to the land of death to see, can one live there? Can one breathe after death has taken one's beloved? How do you cope with overwhelming evil and pain? People ask me: How are you? The question is one from my former world. Now it is one that I cannot answer. I have lost the ability to be in a world where I answer okay. There is no okay. Nothing will ever again be okay. I answer: I'm breathing. I'm alive. But I will never feel relieved, relaxed. Because something will always be missing. I can never again take anything for granted—that the sun will rise, that my husband will return from work. I carry the weight of my son's death everywhere I go, even into my dreams.

Suffering has thrust me into a world where there is no okay. Each moment is a miracle and an agony. A miracle that the world exists in all its glory. An agony that this world is one of suffering and pain. Jewish tradition says that each person is a world. I have lost a whole world.

Chapter six

The Messiah and the Day that Koby was Born

The first sign was the notice about the Messiah. I didn't care very much about it at the time. Still, I put the article in the baby book where I so meticulously recorded Koby's first year of life—like his accomplishment at five weeks: following a tuna fish can with his eyes; his first step at eleven months; his first words at fifteen months. Koby kept this book next to his bed and often looked at it.

In Koby's baby book, an article from the *Jerusalem Post* (June 6, 1987) describes how the week before Koby's birth there were signs posted all over Jerusalem announcing that the Messiah would come to Jerusalem on June 14th. The poster, white lettering on sky blue paper, read: "On Sunday, the 17th of Sivan (June 14, 1987), the Messiah will come to our city. At dawn he will come by way of the Mount of Olives and revive the dead. He will pass through the Gate of Mercy (the Golden Gate) and go up to the Temple Mount. He will climb Mt. Zion and then go to Zion Square, where we will meet him at noon and go to the Knesset. The redeemer will come to Zion and your children will return to your borders."

The article noted that the posters were unsigned and nobody in the municipality knew who had put them up. The *Jerusalem Post* further reported that the Messiah was a no-show. But perhaps they were wrong.

On June 14th, exactly at dawn, 6:07 A.M. to be exact, Koby was born in Jerusalem, as the birds serenaded the world and the sky was streaked with pink, like a baby's cheeks. At the time, I thought it a strange coincidence that my son was born on the day that the posters heralded the Messiah's arrival. I knew nothing about the Messiah. Nor was I interested in him. My husband and I joked together: Sure, we're the parents of the Messiah.

I was a newlywed with a new baby. I thought life was fine, I didn't need another world, or any change in mine. I had no suspicion of the suffering of this world, of the overwhelming need to believe in another world where peace and calm reign, where evil is eradicated, where death is just another state of being, like the new moon, whole and radiant, but invisible to us on earth.

The word messiah means anointed one, and according to Jewish tradition, the Messiah will be the person who God anoints to bring about redemption, to bring peace. This person will lead the world's return to an idyllic time; nations will lay down their swords. Scholar Maurice Lamm states, "It will not be a new world, a qualitatively different world, rather it will be this world brought to perfection."

Jewish tradition states that during the time of the Messiah, the dead will be revived. We're not sure what that will mean exactly, but every day Jews pray to God who is "faithful to resuscitate the dead." At that time, according to some, the righteous will return to their bodies. The body will return to its former wholeness and will then be able to host a totally pure soul. In that state, the body and soul will be perfect, able to perceive everything they weren't able to comprehend when alive in the world. Everything will make sense and the world will be a place of comfort and peace. Spiritual growth will be achieved through joy, instead of through suffering.

In our world, so little makes sense. God's divinity is concealed. When we say the *Shema*, 'Hear O Israel,' the most fundamental Jewish prayer, we cover our eyes in order to concentrate. But covering our eyes is also an admission that we don't know. We are blind in this world, blind to what the truth is. After Koby's death, a rabbi in Monsey, New York, said to me: "We are stupid in this world. We can't see the truth. We can't see the way God works in the world and the purpose of our lives and death. We can't see why Koby was killed. But just as in this world we have many questions and no answers, in the next world we will have no questions, everything will be clear. We will see the other side of the tapestry, not the one with the knots and hanging threads, but the one with the clear beautiful image. As a tailor rips fine material to make a beautiful suit, so, too, we will understand the reason for our rips and tears, our sufferings."

When the Messiah comes, we will see the truth, the wholeness, how everything is connected. And when we see the truth, we will be in a state of awe and grace. The Messiah can arrive any day. We are told that he is ready at any moment to come redeem us. But there are those, like the Trisker Maggid, (Rabbi Avraham Twersky, from the Ukraine, who died in 1889, a Chernobyl Hassid) who say he will not come until we have been aching for him, longing for him, crying out. Until then it is not time for him to come.

The Messiah also waits for us every day. A Jewish legend states that he is an ill beggar sitting at the gates of a city with the other beggars. When the other beggars dress their wounds, they take off all the old bandages and apply ointment. The Messiah doesn't uncover all his sores at once, but one at a time, so that if he is called, he has only one bandage to reapply before rushing to redeem the world. He is wounded and living in a state of readiness. Like me. I am waiting for the Messiah. I cannot live in a world that doesn't allow me the hope of seeing Koby. I can no longer believe in a world of cruelty and evil. I must now believe in another world. Koby's death has catapulted me into belief. So the fact that the advent of the Messiah was predicted in Jerusalem on the day of Koby's birth fills me with awe and hope. It's not that I think Koby was the Messiah. He was a regular kid who collected baseball cards, loved Cal Ripken, and read John Grisham mysteries. But, I now believe, he is part of the process of redeeming and healing the world.

There is meaning in his death and that meaning was pounded into me by the strange set of circumstances surrounding his death and his life. First of all, there was the weather the week before he was murdered. It was as if we received a cosmic warning that all was not right with the world. Nature was not herself. The week before, we'd had a yellow sky after a dust storm. The air was magnetic, charged, filled with dust that filtered the light, coloring the sky a bright, effervescent yellow. I heard people on the radio predicting the end of the world because of the way the sky looked. The next day, dirt rained from the sky, huge gobs of it splattered on the windshields of cars. Then we had a heat wave; then cold; and then rain, even though it hardly ever rains in Israel in May. The weather was confusing, ominous. It filled people with a kind of dread. In Israel the seasons are rigid—rain in the winter, sun in the summer. There are few exceptions and when they occur, we look at them with suspicion.

There are other unusual occurrences associated with Koby's death. Koby died in a cave the week of the holiday of *Lag b'Omer*, when we mark the death of Shimon Bar Yochai, a rabbi from the second century who taught his students the hidden lessons of Jewish mysticism in the Torah. Shimon Bar Yochai spent twelve years with his son learning the secrets of the spiritual world while hiding in a cave, their bodies covered by sand as they studied. Rabbi Menachem Froman, the head rabbi in Tekoa, believes that instead of being up north as is commonly assumed, the cave where Shimon Bar Yochai hid may be in the wadi of Tekoa.

When Koby's friends assembled to dig his grave, they unearthed a powerful sharp-sided hexagonal quartz crystal, extremely rare in this part of Israel. Polished like glass, the rock is pointed like a sword. Koby was killed with coarse boulders, yet in his grave, a rock with perfect symmetry was unearthed.

A week after Koby's death, our house was shot at. The bullet sliced through my daughter's bedroom, skated across her desk, and

28

through a jewelry box. The stone unearthed from Koby's grave, which was also on her desk at the time, was untouched. The only thing left unharmed in the jewelry box was a charm containing the prayer for a safe journey—*tefillat ha'derech,* the Traveler's Prayer.

There are signs and symbols and wonders associated with his death and life. There are connections I don't understand. I am part of a story that is larger than myself. Koby's death reaches past the length of my arms and legs; it snakes out toward the world and demands to be explored.

My purpose now is to hold Koby's death in my hands, to cradle his life and death, and turn it like a quartz crystal to reveal each facet of light within, each particle of holiness, each ray of hope.

I falter at times. I fall into grief. I despair at meaning. What is meaning with my son gone? And then the wave of pain passes. I swim toward his life and death, reaching again for meaning, a raft that will keep me from drowning.

Chapter seven

Elijah's Appearance at Koby's Circumcision

F irst there were posters declaring the arrival of the Messiah. Next came Elijah the Prophet's appearance at Koby's circumcision ceremony in a restaurant in downtown Jerusalem. Our friend Roger saw him. But I didn't believe him then.

I wasn't the signs and wonders type. I'd had an Ivy League education and wasn't looking for signs from God. I didn't grow up religious. In fact, I'd had no religious education, no Sunday school, no Hebrew school, and no *Bat Mitzvah*. My father wasn't interested in the synagogue in our town. He said it was too much of a fashion show. My mother and her mother had had no Jewish education. My grandmother used to make me bacon sandwiches for lunch. I'd worked at the temple as a busgirl, setting tables, pouring water and folding napkins, wearing red velvet hot pants. I knew I was Jewish, but I didn't know very much about what that meant. I'd never met an observant Jew, never even heard about *Shabbat*.

Being Jewish was something I wanted to get rid of. It didn't seem so positive being a Jew. It seemed like a burden.

At my elementary school in East Rockaway on Long Island, 98 percent of the kids were Jewish, and almost all of them went to Hebrew School. I thought it was great that while they were in Hebrew school in the afternoon, I could come home and watch TV. I celebrated my thirteenth birthday by going with my parents to *Hair*—which had a nude scene—on Broadway, dancing at the end on stage with the cast. In ninth grade, I was a cheerleader.

I didn't rebel against my parents in high school. They were very easy going, and they didn't dictate how I should be. But in my twenties, my rebellion took the form of a search for meaning. I traveled to Israel in 1984 because I wanted to work on a kibbutz. I'd read about them in college, written a paper on child-raising on kibbutz. The ideology of kibbutz life appealed to me: the idealism, the collective spirit. But I also went to Israel because I felt like something was missing in my being. I'd gone to Cornell and then Colorado State where I got a Masters in Creative Writing. I was a poet. I connected to the spirituality in poetry; a metaphor was, in essence, a re-visioning of the world, a way of saying that things that you thought weren't connected could be. A rock could be compared to death; water disappearing down a drain could be a flower. That which was different was in essence the same. There was a kind of unity to the universe.

Then I went to California, to L.A., and worked on 'The Dinner Party Project'—a feminist art project which opened at the San Francisco Museum of Modern Art, created by Judy Chicago with the help of almost one hundred volunteers. The project was a room-sized retelling of women's history, complete with women's crafts, like dinner plates sculpted in vaginal images. A volunteer, I embroidered the runners, tablecloths that were under each important woman's place setting. The embroidery represented the woman's outer life. I became disillusioned with feminism after Judy Chicago yelled at me for disturbing her when she had a phone call. I thought feminists should at least be nice, that the power hierarchy would change in a feminist project. But I saw that in the end, she was a boss like any other.

Later I got my first full time job at Virginia Commonwealth University. I was teaching freshman composition and in a story we read, the Jewish holiday of *Chanukah*, the festival of lights, was mentioned. I realized that I was the only Jew in the room, and yet I couldn't explain to the class the real story of *Chanukah*. Of course, I knew that we lit candles, but I didn't know exactly who the Maccabees were, or why they were fighting.

In 1984, after my teaching job ended, I moved to Granada in Spain, where I lived in a house hewn out of a cave with no electricity. I studied Spanish, translated poetry, and listened to the gypsies, who lived near me, play flamenco. I was planning to go to Australia to visit my boyfriend, who was a cowboy working on a ranch in the Outback. When, instead, we broke up, I figured it wouldn't hurt to learn more about what it meant to be Jewish. And as somebody who had only gone out with non-Jewish guys, I thought that maybe it was time to try dating somebody Jewish.

In 1984, I arrived in Israel. After living in Spain, I felt immediately at home. I'd never adjusted to the way people ate and dressed in Spain. When I wanted breakfast, all I could find was coffee. Then there'd be a huge lunch, and dinner wasn't until 10:00 P.M. I didn't feel in sync with the people or the culture either. I didn't feel welcome there. So coming to Israel felt like a relief. I was supposed to stay with a friend from college, but she was away, so I stayed with her husband, Jon Medved, who took me around the Old City as if he personally had designed it. He was so proud of Jerusalem. "Taste these olives, taste these tomatoes. There are no tomatoes like these in America, are there?" he asked me.

People were happy that I was in Israel. People that I met casually would say—"Stay, you're home."

After a while, I went to kibbutz as a volunteer. I was already twenty-eight; most of the volunteers were twenty. It turned out I wasn't interested in waking before dawn, working in a vineyard and partying all night. I left after a week. Then I went to Safed, a beautiful town in Northern Israel, and began to study at *Livnot U'Lehibanot* ('To Build and to be Built'), a program that combines Jewish studies with volunteer community work.

I loved learning, trying to unravel texts; I liked the feeling of continuity, the feeling of significance. I learned that there were Jewish mystics who had lived in Granada before the Spanish Inquisition, but that Jewish mysticism began to flourish only later, in the northern Israeli city of Safed, well after the Jews were expelled from Spain and Portugal in 1492. Not only were the mystics interested in their own transcendence, but they questioned the meaning of the suffering the Jews had experienced during the Inquisition.

In some strange way, I was unwittingly traveling a similar journey, at least geographically. But I wasn't interested in being religious, keeping kosher, or keeping the laws of the Sabbath. I stayed in the program but moved into my own apartment in Safed. I wasn't interested in the rules of religion, but I was entranced with its spirit. After that program, a friend offered me a free room in Jerusalem because he would be in the army. I moved to Jerusalem to study basic Hebrew and another friend introduced me to Seth.

Seth is from Willimantic, Connecticut, a small mill town thirty-five miles east of Hartford. When his father, Jack, (after whom Koby is named) was five, he almost got run over in the Lower East Side of New York by a wagon. The family decided to move up to the country where they'd vacationed previously. His grandfather started the synagogue. When Seth was growing up, his family was one of about one hundred Jewish families in a town of 15,000. There were eight kids in Seth's Hebrew school class. His father was a baker, his mother a homemaker. Seth is the youngest of three brothers; his two older brothers are now lawyers who live in small towns, not so dissimilar to Willimantic. Seth went to college nearby, the University of Connecticut. Afterwards, he couldn't wait to leave Connecticut.

He was planning on going to New Orleans to become a bartender. But when John Chancellor announced in 1973 on the NBC evening news that Israel was at war and needed volunteers to work on the kibbutzim, he decided that it would be more fun to go to Israel.

Seth worked on kibbutzim and later was on his way to the Peace Corps in Senegal when he met a rabbi who encouraged him to study. "You're open to everything else, why not be open to your own tradition?" he asked Seth. Seth went to the *yeshiva* for a day, and found it interesting. He returned a few months later, and instead of going to the Peace Corps, began an intensive course of study in the *yeshiva*. He was no longer in the *yeshiva* when I met him. Although he was still studying by himself, still learning Talmud and Jewish philosophy, he was ready to leave religion—when I was just getting interested in it. We met in the middle.

Part of my attraction to Seth was that his religion made him seem curiously exotic to me. But he was also similar. He was from a small town in Connecticut, and we later found out that our parents both had chosen to live in the same condo in Florida. He was like the boy next door, only transplanted. I realized that while I usually was attracted to men I couldn't ever really know well because they were so different from me (like my cowboy boyfriend), I felt like I could get to know him, and that we could grow together.

I found Judaism fascinating and my husband's interest and knowledge captivated me. I even found his praying attractive, almost sexy. It was beautiful to be captivated by something, to find meaning in something, to believe in something so fully. I immediately recognized the deep wisdom in Judaism. After years of being embarrassed of being Jewish, I understood that being Jewish was a gift I had never opened.

When I got married in 1985 in Jerusalem, I agreed to keep the Sabbath (*Shabbat*), *kashrut*, and the laws of *niddah* (abstaining from touching one's spouse during menstruation), but I had no idea of the enormity of what I had taken on. I kept my promise to Seth, but I also sometimes rebelled, flipping on the lights on *Shabbat*, for example, when according to Orthodox practice, switching on electricity is forbidden because of the prohibition against lighting a fire. At times I felt imprisoned by Jewish law—and by Seth. In a way, I'd been seduced into religious practice, and it took me years to accept all that I had taken on, to integrate it, to know who I was as a religious person. Seth also learned to accept me more as I was, not as he wanted me to be.

I had no idea how Koby's death would one day shake the nest we'd created, and how fortunate I would be to be with a man I could understand and hold on to.

So even though I was 'religious' when my son was born, I didn't have a strong belief system. I liked the lifestyle of Jewish observance—*Shabbat*, the holidays, the feeling of community, the emphasis on study—and what I especially liked was the congruence between what people studied and how they behaved. Though not perfect, people were working on being more giving, more caring, more concerned about others.

Belief in God, though, was a problem. I just wasn't a believer. It didn't come naturally to me. I could believe in God intellectually, but emotionally, he didn't exist for me. Seth told me that he had had the same problem and the rabbis had told him to go to the Western Wall for thirty days in a row, pray for belief, and then act as if he did believe and eventually belief would come. Seth said it had worked for him and he now believed in God. But his wasn't an emotional believing. It made sense that the world had a creator. I understood the logic—it was as probable that there was a God as there wasn't. And since everything else had a creator, even the garbage bag in my kitchen, it seemed reasonable that there was a creator of the world. But I wanted more feeling in my belief and it just wasn't there. I didn't feel any sign of God.

So at Koby's circumcision, I wasn't thinking about God or the Messiah or Elijah, who is said to attend each *brit mila,* the circumcision ceremony that reminds us that even the most earthy, material and profane organ can be used for holiness. The ceremony is seen as perfecting the baby and joining him to the covenant of God. God commands that the *brit* be on the eighth day, perhaps because eight is a number that is above nature. God created the world in six days, on the seventh he rested; and the eighth day is a day when God ceased both his material and spiritual work. The number eight takes us out of this world Into the realm of the infinite and divine, into the world of miracles.

But I wasn't thinking about miracles or the long line of Jewish babies who'd been circumcised for thousands and thousands of years. I was thinking that I was in pain from the long delivery. Since there was a transportation strike in Jerusalem, we had to walk the ten minutes in the heat to the restaurant, Off the Square, in downtown Jerusalem for the ceremony and I hurt like hell. Even though I'd had a natural delivery, without an episiotomy, I had a small tear, and I was in pain.

"Look," Seth said. "The signs are still up." The signs announcing the Messiah's arrival. Sure enough. June 14th, at sunrise. I looked at my baby in his carriage, his features so perfect, his sleep so gentle and exquisite. I had my baby. What did I need with a messiah?

I also didn't need Elijah, though he was an unexpected guest at the *brit*. Elijah is said to descend from heaven and transform himself in order to help people or perform miracles. He is considered the prophet who never dies. He ascended alive to heaven in a chariot of fire and returns to earth whenever he is needed, to help those in distress. He can appear in any form, old or young, rich or poor, in dreams or waking visions. He saves poor starving families from misery; he rescues whole communities from disaster. His soul, though, is too big to be contained on earth, so he needs to return to heaven from time to time to visit and reconnect, recharge. Sometimes he is referred to as the bird of heaven, flying back and forth, at home in both heaven and earth.

In every generation, Elijah reveals himself. Not only does he perform miracles, saving righteous people from death, but it is said that he will also herald the Messiah's arrival, revealing himself one day before the coming of the Messiah. He is the one who will cause the belief of God to spread on earth.

Elijah has to witness each Jewish *brit*, because in his zealousness he once spoke against the Jewish people, accusing them of abandoning God's commandment to circumcise each Jewish baby. Instead of believing God when He told him that the Jews were performing the *mitzvot*, his commandments, Elijah acted like a prosecutor, unable to revise his verdict. He told God to punish the Jews by not sending His healing dew to the earth. God responded by requiring that Elijah see that the Jews were still performing the ritual of circumcision. Elijah's *tikkun*—a word that means to be fixed or repaired—was to witness every Jewish *brit*, so that he would never again speak out against the people. In fact, he is supposed to report to God each circumcision and each good deed that a Jew performs.

Once I thought living forever like Elijah, the bird of heaven, would be a privilege. But now I see it differently. It is not necessarily a merit to live forever; to fly between heaven and earth. Elijah never gets to rest. Because he was so stubborn, a zealot with an angry temper, adolescent in his inability to see another person's view, another way of being, he is forced to keep encountering the goodness in people, perhaps so he can recognize it in himself.

Elijah kept his word and was a guest at Koby's *brit*. We have a photograph of Elijah at the time of the circumcision. An elderly, distinguished looking stranger, he walked into the restaurant where we held the circumcision ceremony. Elijah is wearing a gray suit, a black *kippah*, seated next to Seth, while the crowd of onlookers stand; he looks as if he knows his place at the *brit*.

We didn't realize he was a beggar until he asked Seth for charity. Seth gave him a small amount, and I saved the receipt in Koby's baby book. When we looked at the receipt after Koby's death and read the fine print we realized that the money was being collected for the students of the yeshiva of Rabbi Shimon Bar Yochai—the rabbi associated with Kaballah and Jewish mysticism, the rabbi who studied for twelve years in a cave, whose death we commemorate on *Lag b'Omer*.

Our friend Roger noticed Elijah at the *brit*, because our Elijah had a long white beard and was wearing a large black belt. In the *Book of Kings*, we learn that Elijah was a hairy man who girded himself with a girdle of leather about his loins. The significance of the belt in Chassidic sources is that it separates the body, and distinguishes between the holy parts, the head, chest and hands, which according to the Talmud, are created in the image of God, and the lower part of the body. In his book, *Nine Gates to the Chassidic Mysteries*, Jiri Langer says, "In the lower part (of the body), with its functions of digestion and secretion, a man is similar to an animal. The belt thus demarcates the boundary between the Godly part and the animal part of a man..."

Roger also noticed Elijah's avuncular concern, and wanted to know who he was. Elijah stood up front, as close to the rabbi holding the baby as possible, fingering his long white beard. At the end of the ceremony, Roger followed Elijah out the door. Roger got on his motorcycle, and when the man turned left down a narrow alley, Roger turned left. When the man turned right, Roger turned right. And when Roger looked up the street, Elijah had disappeared.

Of course then, when Roger told us the story, we didn't think the beggar was Elijah. But now we do. Because Elijah wasn't just there when Koby was born. He was there also on the day he died. Before Koby and Yosef were murdered, they first went to the little food store in our town. Our town has only about two hundred and fifty families so Rena and Jacob Aiyokai, the owners of the store, know just about everyone. On that same morning, Rena said, she noticed an older gentleman with a white beard whom she had never seen before in the store. Yosef was in the store, buying food for their expedition. He told Rena that he was cutting school and going to the wadi. Rena told him to go to school, that she would give him a ride later. Koby was presumably waiting outside, hiding so that nobody would see that he hadn't gone to school, since he knew he would get into trouble with me if I heard about it. The man began to talk to Yosef, telling him not to go to the wadi. We think it was Elijah, trying to warn the boys. Perhaps Elijah also stepped outside to talk to Koby. But Koby and Yosef were teenagers, and even Elijah couldn't save them. There were no miracles that day.

I cry to God, to Elijah. You perform so many miracles: Why didn't you save them? Why didn't you protect my son? Why didn't you return Koby to me with just a broken leg or even a concussion? Why did you have to take my son?

I don't have any answers. I imagine Elijah going up to heaven, saying that he did what he could: he witnessed the circumcision and he tried to save the boys. Elijah, I want more than a message. I want a miracle.

Chapter eight

The World-to-Come

W hy was Koby chosen? Why were we? Even Job, the righteous man, could not contain himself and questioned God, railing against his suffering. Every rabbi I go to tells me not to ask that question. I will never know why in this world. There are no whys. There is only for what. What can I do in the aftermath of Koby's murder? Still I wonder. And I am given clues.

One clue has to do with Yosef and Koby's friendship. They were an odd pair. They both arrived in Tekoa the same year. The family of Yosef Ish-Ran moved to Tekoa from Jerusalem, twelve miles away; our family from Efrat, near Tekoa, but before that, from Silver Spring, Maryland, a suburb of Washington D.C., halfway around the world. Yosef was native born; his mother, Rena, is a nurse who works in the emergency room in Hadassah Hospital, his father, Ezra, is a policeman. Rena's parents are from Iran, Ezra's are from Turkey, traditional God-fearing Jews, although Rena and Ezra are less observant. Koby was a new immigrant with a rabbi and a writer for parents—newly-religious Jews who had met in Israel, moved back to the States for seven years, and then returned to Israel five years before the murder.

Koby and Yosef were different in temperament as well. Koby loved to read and be at home; he was often shy outside of the house. He was self-conscious about his Hebrew, which he spoke with an American accent. Although he'd moved to Israel in fourth grade, he was still American, with American interests. He read for pleasure in English. He kept up with American sports, and still collected baseball cards. He was brilliant in school and had a photographic memory, so he did well despite his difficulties with Hebrew. Native-born, Yosef was a charmer, very social, always out talking to people. He was more gregarious than Koby, did less well in school. And he wasn't religiously observant.

I was happy that Koby had found a friend, especially one with whom he spoke only Hebrew. In fact, my son Daniel said that sometimes when we would send Yosef home at night because it was late, Yosef would stay outside in the garden, talking to Koby from outside his window.

They each had a love of laughter. One of the things that must have drawn Koby and Yosef together was their sense of humor. After their murder, I found a floppy disk of jokes Koby had collected. The first line of that file is Yosef's email address. Koby and I would spend much of our time together laughing, with him telling me jokes. I remember his delight in telling his first joke at the *Shabbat* table at the age of eight—a long joke about a Cohen who doesn't realize that you become a Cohen by being born one. When he got older, he told a whole set of jokes ranging from 'your mama's so fat' to rabbi jokes. He shared his jokes with everybody.

Why were these particular boys chosen? Nobody can know. But I believe there is a hint in a story related in the Babylonian Talmud (*Ta'anit 22a*) about Elijah and the World-to-Come.

One day Elijah was in the marketplace. Rabbi Beroka strode up to him and said: "Show me somebody with *olam ha ba*—somebody who will attain the World-to-Come." Rabbi Beroka meant—show me somebody who has earned the right to live forever because he or she is on such a high level of godliness; show me somebody who will bask in God's radiance, who will be God's beloved. There were many Talmud scholars in the market, impeccably dressed in long robes and turbans. Rabbi Beroka thought that surely these men with their great learning would merit God's light and eternal life. Elijah shook his head no and said, "I'm sorry. There's nobody here like that." Rabbi Beroka stroked his beard in surprise. Then a pair of young men entered the market, talking and laughing, dressed in worn out, simple clothes. Elijah pointed to them and said: "Those men merit to live forever."

Rabbi Beroka went up to them and asked: "You merit to live forever. Why? Why you?"

The young men knew why. They responded: "We tell jokes and make sad people happy. We bring people together in peace with laughter."

At Jewish weddings, there used to be a storyteller, a *badchan*, whose job it was to bring cheer to the bride and groom. Koby, to me, was like that storyteller. If I was having a hard day, Koby noticed. Sometimes, he would bring me a drink. But he always made sure to fill it to the tippy-top so that it spilled a little, and made me laugh because it was so hard to drink. Koby was always surprising me.

Koby and Yosef loved to laugh, loved to be happy. But why is making people happy such an important value? Why does happiness bring the World-to-Come? Rabbi Nachman, a nineteenth century rabbi from the Ukraine, explains that being joyous is not just a right but also an obligation. Rabbi Nachman also had a child die. He understood that in being happy, we give ourselves strength. We believe that our lives have meaning and purpose, and that God gives us challenges so that we can grow. Rabbi Nachman says that it is a person's nature to be drawn into melancholy and sadness. When we struggle to be joyous we recognize and affirm God's presence in the world, his essential goodness. It is said that the prophets had to be joyous to receive God's word. God dwells in joy.

I want Koby next to me, laughing. Instead I imagine Yosef and Koby up in heaven. They are telling jokes to each other, telling jokes to God. Perhaps God took the boys because he, himself, needed to be cheered up.

Chapter nine

Potato Chips at the Funeral

Y our funeral is no more real to me than a fire made of water, than an ocean made of stone. My friends in New York see us on TV, my body bowed over your coffin. But I don't believe, and I will never believe, that you are in the cemetery.

We begin the funeral procession in our town. The wind has been blowing all day, ferociously, so strong that friends help me find my winter coat, which is already packed away, so that I can wear it to the cemetery. I step out of the house and have to hold on to my friends because the wind is pushing me back. The social worker has designated an adult responsible for each of my children. They walk alongside us to the main road in our town. I hold my kids' hands. People line the street. There is an ambulance and a line of cars. Where is Koby's body I wonder. Where is my son?

As soon as the funeral procession begins, the wind dies down. I hold my husband, my children, my friends. The rabbi's wife takes a knife and slices a rip in my shirt from the collar, rends my husband's shirt and my children's as well. The tear is like the tear in my heart. I do not faint but my legs don't want to accept the weight of my body; my body wants to collapse, wants to plunge to the earth; wants to disappear. But I don't.

I feel like my heart has stopped: this moment is the moment that will stand as forever in my life.

Somebody brings me a folding chair and medics take my pulse. The rabbi speaks. I look out and see the pale gray color of the wadi, the rugged cliffs. I stand and hold my children. I don't hear a word that the rabbi says. Somebody gives me a drink of water. Cameras push their way toward me like burrowing animals, trying to expose my pain. I walk to a car and as soon as I get in the back seat, I scream at the horror and the pain and the fact that I am in a car with my husband and three innocent children and we are on our way to bury their brother. There is a long procession of cars. We drive through an Arab village and then we pass the neighboring town of Efrat. Throngs of people fill the road. We drive through them and they part for us like the Red Sea. They are praying, heads down, bowed. They have come to say goodbye to Koby and Yosef. Later, I am told that they have waited for hours.

We stop at a junction for a public ceremony before proceeding to the cemetery. Thousands of people join us. Limor Livnat, the Minister of Education, and some other politicians speak, and I see two stretchers on metal stands. I can't breathe. I had no idea that my son's body would be laid out here, exposed. On top of each stand is a body wrapped in a *tallit*, a prayer shawl. Written on a tag at the bottom of the stretcher is the name: Koby Mandell. This is the last day I will see my son, and this is the last touch I will give him. I lay my face on top of his body and wonder where is his head; where are his legs? He is so tightly wrapped I can't tell. I hold him and try to hug him and remember how the nurses swaddled him tightly when he was born, bound him so he would feel secure. And now he is swaddled again, and I hold him and feel nothing, and suddenly I understand death. He is a body without a spirit. I know his soul has gone somewhere else; is no longer with us. There is a huge throng of people but I am alone with my son's death. Take me into the earth, I would like to pray. But there is something in me that keeps me upright, that keeps me walking, that keeps me alive. The life force that led me to my closet to pick out an outfit for the funeral; the life force that keeps me from collapsing. We get back in the car. A convoy of cars containing Rena and Ezra and their family drives away from us to the Har HaMenuchot cemetery in Jerusalem. Our friend Avraham drives us to the cemetery in Kfar Etzion. I think: I can't bear this; I can't live anymore. I don't know how I will live with evil; how I will explain evil to my children; how we will live with death as our companion, how we will live without Koby.

We arrive at the cemetery and are about to open the doors of the car. This is a moment of sheer terror for me, pain that is so intense that I feel that my soul has also left my body. I am disconnected from my limbs, from my heart, my breathing. A mother should not have to watch her son put into the ground. A mother should die before her child. A mother should not have to bear witness to the terrible fact that much as she loves her child, she can't protect him; she can't save him from a death so brutal we had to provide dental records so that my son and Yosef could be told apart.

I wonder where I will find the strength to walk to the grave. As I open the car door, Gavi, my six-year-old son says: "I'm hungry. I'm hungry, Mommy."

"What?" I ask. "Didn't anybody feed you?"

"No, I'm hungry," he says.

A policeman makes an emergency run, siren blaring, to a nearby market and brings Gavi potato chips and we remain by the car as he eats. Hunger. Simple hunger. Even at the moment of death. Even at the most tragic, cruelest hour of life, God is pulling me out of my pain by giving me a son who is alive and hungry. God is reminding me that life is all around me, even here, surrounded by dead souls. Gavi is crunching potato chips, enjoying them.

There is a life force that makes us breathe, that calls us to look up to the stars at the most tragic moments. There is a life force that demands our attention. As Rachel Naomi Remen, a doctor who has done extensive work with cancer patients, says in *Kitchen Table Wisdom*: "That tendency toward life endures in all of us, undiminished, until the moment of our death." Though it may be impermanent, life is not fragile. The drive to life is strong.

We walk down to the graveyard. The darkness is a gift that keeps me from seeing too clearly. Thousands of people surround the grave and fill the space between the grave and the parking lot overlooking the graves. Without having told us, my eleven-year-old son delivers a eulogy, crying out to the crowd in the midst of his tears. He tells Koby: "I wanted you to be there when I got home. What will I do without you, my best friend? Who will tell me what to do? Who will I laugh with? Who will I talk to? How could they have killed you, a thirteen-year-old boy?"

Rabbis speak. Koby's teacher speaks. A friend speaks. I hold on to Eliana and Gavi as my husband speaks. "This is not our script," he says. "This is not the story we came here for. We came here to be close to God. We wanted to be part of Jewish history but we forget what Jewish history means, we forgot the suffering and murder that are part of our history. I remember when you were a baby, I used to hold you as I studied and learned the words of the Talmud and I hoped that the holy words would enter you and fill your being. As you got older, I taught you and taught you. But there's one thing I never taught you—how to die."

I hear without listening. I see with my eyes closed. My son's shrouded body is lowered into the ground. As in all traditional burials in Israel, there is no coffin because we want the body to naturally return to the earth, to the dust. We don't want to impede the process of separating the body from the soul, because the body needs to go through a period of purification so that one day, in the time of the resurrection, in a new form, the body can be reunited with the soul. The men begin to shovel dirt over my son and people line up to toss rocks on the open grave.

I am at someone else's funeral, someone I don't know. I don't cry. I walk up to the parking lot, a procession of men standing on either side of me, lining our walk back to the car. They chant a prayer and I walk past them and through the darkness, my friends holding my weight as my body collapses into itself. I feel nothing. Because Koby is not here. Koby is nowhere near this grave. Koby is not in the air and Koby is not in the ground. I would know if he were here.

He would be poking me with his elbow or shouting in my ear. He would be lifting me up to show me how strong he is. He would be stepping on my toes to get my attention. He would put his arm around me and hug me. I would feel him.

Chapter ten

The *Shiva* and the Faces of God

I t is as if I have left my body. My husband and I have become one body, one soul, joined together in our pain, alone with our pain together. That first night we sleep a few hours, wake at 4:00 A.M. and go out to the terrace off our bedroom. The birds are singing, it is growing light, the sky is streaked with purple and pink, and we wrap our arms around each other and cry together.

My husband remembers friends of his who died young. I remember waking up with Koby when he was a baby early in the morning, nursing him. The birds sang loudly, sweeping across the sky. It was a secret, magic time, a time alone with my baby when the true beauty of the world was revealed to me.

This morning I hear the birds again. The sound is so loud, it seems like a texture, something you can touch, like a thick blanket over us. The sound is a sign telling me that the ordinary life we knew is being transformed; intangible sound has suddenly become material, tangible. We are not just one form but can be transformed; matter transmuting itself into spirit and back. Death is a permutation, a change of form. Rimbaud wrote about different senses merging in poetry. Touch and sound have merged, as synesthesia is made manifest for me.

The moon still in the sky looks like the opening of a tunnel, calling me to believe that my son is on a journey to a land I cannot yet know. I want to hold his hand, and yank him back to me. I want to say to him: Did you take a jacket? Did you take water? Did you eat? I want to take care of him.

My husband and I stand together in a kind of tenderness that we haven't felt in years, perhaps never. We are fully present for each other. Koby has given the gift of a bond that feels necessary, urgent, a life support system that will keep us alive.

Later that day, Gavi asks me: "Who is Koby's mommy, now?"

I wonder what to answer. It's true that I am still Koby's mommy, but I am no longer the one who takes care of him. I answer, "God is his mommy."

"Oh good," answers Gavi. "Then he can see a falling star whenever he wants."

My child believes in the goodness of the world. My child believes in magic. My child believes in God.

Ҙ

During the seven days of mourning, the *shiva*, I live in the land of pain. My friends fear I won't return to myself, that I won't have the strength to go on. Seth worries about me because my eyes swing in their sockets; I can't eat. My friends beg me to eat. They rub my shoulders and my back. They try to spoon baby food into my mouth. The doctor comes and checks my tongue, my blood pressure. He tells me I must eat. But food is for people who are alive, and I am not. I get up and go downstairs and cry out in my pain. I sit on the floor and am cradled by thousands of people who reach out to me. My children join me on the floor; they are in their rooms with friends; they play upstairs, I don't know who is taking care of them but I see them eating. I see adults surrounding them. I speak to them and hold them, but they prefer to be with their friends. My pain is a flame that they can feel in my hands, see in my eyes.

Seven days of mourning. The mirrors are covered. Vanity is a luxury in the midst of such pain. One wants to forget the material world, be transformed into a spirit so that one can merge with the dead. This world seems like a world of shadow. The body is insubstantial. I don't want to perform my rituals of vanity—the quick dab of eye makeup, lipstick. I don't bathe. I wear the same ripped shirt all week. Breathing is all I can manage. Most people can't tolerate a mourner's silence, and rush to fill it, but Jewish mourning laws dictate that a person paying a *shiva* call should be silent until the mourner speaks. If the mourner says nothing, the person visiting should say nothing as well. Neither should greet each other. The first three days, when the pain is most intense, the mourner is like an egg, without a mouth, dwelling in silence. The point of the *shiva* is not to comfort a mourner for her loss but to stand with her in the time of her grief. As Rabbi Maurice Lamm notes, the main purpose of the *shiva* is to relieve the mourner of his loneliness. A person expresses compassion for the mourner through his presence and silence. Job sat with his friends for seven days and none uttered a sound. For only God can comfort. That is why, when departing a *shiva*, many traditional Jews state these words: "May God comfort you among the mourners of Zion and Jerusalem." But I am not silent. I need to talk about Koby. I cannot contain the pain of silence.

And there are people who come and offer me words that ease my loneliness. Not formulaic statements like—'he's in a better place', or 'thank God you have your other children', but words that tell me that they can stand with us in this place of sorrow. I need to speak. I need people to talk to me. I ask my friend to put a sign on a door-this is a house of *shiva* and all conversation should be about Koby. I refuse to listen to anything trite, anything mundane. I tell people: only Koby, only Koby.

There are many people who offer me wisdom, and I hold on to their words like a rope that I can climb. The women bend down to me, sitting on the floor, putting their faces to mine. Their faces are so beautiful—their eyes open, their voices soft and strong. Today I know that each person is created in the image of God, because I see and hear God in their faces, the faces of God. I know all of these women are God coming to comfort me, their arms wrapped around me; their eyes looking into mine. They reach into their souls and give me divine pieces of themselves; love and compassion—they feed me with their words. Israeli women are unafraid of suffering; they know death as a companion. They say:

"Your son will not be forgotten. We will not let him be forgotten..."

"We will be with you. You will never be alone, never..."

"He is our son too; we are crying with you...."

"He is with God and he is basking in God's love and you will bask in our love..."

"Your son is like a boat, a beautiful boat sailing and when it goes over the horizon you won't be able to see it, but it's still there, sailing along the open waters...."

And this: "My brother was killed and my mother suffered but after the terrible pain, there were gifts. My mother was a Holocaust survivor, her parents and brothers and sisters were killed in the war. She made a new life here in Israel. Then my brother was killed in a terrorist attack on a bus in 1979." I remember this. I once stayed at this woman's house for *Shabbat*, and all night, the picture of the handsome young man in the photograph looked down at me, and I felt he had died. In the morning, I asked her, and she told me that her brother had died when he was twenty-six. She says: "My mother had great blessings in her life, even with her misfortune, and so will you. God takes away, but he also gives. You will receive. God will give you *bracha*."

These words move me, and I want to believe them. But I don't understand them.

The mothers who have lost children to terrorism arrive. One, who lost her teenage son in an attack when he was hiking in Wadi Kelt, says: "You will go on. You will live." She gives me practical advice: "Don't make a shrine for your son. Pack up his things and put them away. Use his room. You don't need to keep out his pictures everywhere."

She is an attractive woman, her hair styled in a fashionable, short cut. She is wearing makeup, earrings. I look at her and realize: You can still be alive after your son is dead.

A woman who lost her nineteen-year-old son in a drive-by shooting, says: "He is not gone. He will live inside of you now. We miss their physical bodies but we are still tied to them. You will never forget him."

I reach out for their hands like branches that will pull me across a raging river. One of my friends tells me: "You are all soul, you are letting us see your soul."

The politicians arrive. Israel is a small country with a history of conflict, and there is a custom of politicians attending the funeral or the *shiva* of each person killed by terror or war, each person killed by a national enemy. I tell the President, Moshe Katzav—I need a father to comfort me. He stares at me without seeing me. The chief rabbi, the ministers, the mayors…none of them have the right words of comfort for me.

"What do we do with the pain?" my husband asks a rabbi who, years ago, lost his eleven-year-old child in a bus accident. The rabbi answers: "You must use it to grow."

Another rabbi says that ours is a heartbreaking test, but we need to turn to God, that only God can give us comfort. Outside of the house, my friend Valerie tells me, the rabbis cry like babies.

Because no matter how much we try to intellectualize or interpret the pain, to will it away, the pain crouches on our heart like a beast who is waiting to crush us, to chew us to bits until we are nothing, dust that the wind can blow away.

I wake up each morning crying and I go to sleep in tears. My body is a poor companion now. It is too material. I want to peel it away, find the soul inside and merge with my son.

I look at the women who wrap their arms around me, who give me their bodies to cry on. They are my Yemenite and Moroccan and Portuguese and American mothers. There is so much love in that *shiva*, so much love; the love lifts me up and keeps me afloat like I am a body being carried.

Chapter eleven

The Canyon
and the Spring

Everybody has a landscape that suits their inner being. Some need the lights of the city; some need green fields; some need to live by the sea. Many of us never dwell in the landscape that suits us. We live somewhere and our soul protests. It longs for something that it recognizes as its own.

We knew we belonged in Tekoa the moment we saw the wadi, the gorge cutting through the canyon in the Judean desert. It was as if we were home. The beauty was breathtaking—a series of striated mountains that seemed to stretch into infinity flanking a snaking gorge—a riverbed that sliced through unyielding rock. Brown and gray and sand blue, colors merge so that it's hard to tell where the ground leaves off and the sky begins. The landscape here drew us to it—as if we were parched for it. Its barrenness called to us. Although the landscape here is monumental, it doesn't boast, isn't proud of itself. It is humble in its magnificence.

The people in Tekoa are pretty much the same—humble and

down to earth, and yet many are grand in their spirit. There are immigrants here from all over the world—Russia and France, Argentina, and Morocco—and native Israelis as well.

Tekoa was first set up in the mid 1970s as an army outpost and was then established as a settlement in 1977 by Rabin's Labor government, with Shimon Peres one of its main supporters. At first, it was a secular settlement populated by a small number of new Russian immigrants. Slowly other groups of people from France and America joined them. In 1978, the Russian founders made the decision that, though they weren't religious, they believed it was important that their children be exposed to Jewish tradition. Consequently, they decided that the mandate of the community would state that Tekoa was a place for religious and secular Jews to live together.

At first, relations with the Arabs were very good. But then David Rosenfeld, a young American immigrant, was killed by terrorists in 1982 while working in Herodion, a fortress about a mile from Tekoa. During the Intifada in the late 1980s, it was common for cars to be stoned. In 1987, Mordechai Lipkin, a painter, was killed on the road to Jerusalem. By the time we arrived in Tekoa in 1998, things were quiet but there was little interchange between Arabs and Jews. We moved to Tekoa because we liked the community, not because we wanted to be settlers. It was after Oslo; we thought that we could live in peace.

If you came here, you probably wouldn't look at the people here and think first—settler. You would be surprised at the relaxed life we lead and the freedom our children experience. The school in Tekoa, for example, is unusual because both religious and non-religious kids learn together. The children learn through action and experience as well as study. The children plant wheat seeds and then they grow, pick, and grind the wheat, transforming it into flour, baking bread themselves. Then they learn the commandments associated with growing wheat and baking bread, including tithing, separating *challah*, and making a blessing. The children learn to plant and grow, to compost; they keep animals like goats, donkeys, and rabbits. They pick sage and learn that you can clean your teeth with it; they pick olives from the trees here and pickle them. Tekoa is a village like the one Hillary Clinton describes when she says—"it takes a village to raise a child." If a small child on his way to school here cries because he forgot his sandwich, another mother will hear him and make him one. My son Daniel once said it felt like each house in Tekoa was the room of one big house and he could go into any room he wanted.

It is a place where you can be religious and live a rural life. There is a vineyard, a mushroom farm, olive groves, horses. And it is stunningly beautiful. The opening to the trail in the gorge is a five-minute walk from our home. We used to hike there and watch our children jump assuredly like gazelles while we stepped our way down and up the steep outcroppings of rock. In the caves where monks lived during the fifth century, we used to stop and retrieve ancient shards of pottery from the ground.

Being in the wadi is like being at sea. You can see the way time has worked, sculpting the rugged mountains; water and earthquakes carve their impressions, creating a series of caves, including the Haritun Cave, one of the largest in the Middle East. It is almost as if time is stored here.

I have a picture of Koby standing at the edge of the wadi. He and I and some of my women friends had gone hiking a year before his murder. He has his arms up; he's laughing, shouting, proud of himself, a boy against a background of the infinite. Rough terrain, rugged outcroppings of rock, fossils, shards of pottery, shadows and light and caves—you couldn't ask for more to keep a boy interested.

The silence in the wadi is an ancient silence, so overwhelming that it is almost a presence, a sound. Perhaps it is the sound of God. It feels that way to me. I feel that I am in the presence of majesty, of glory. As the explanation for one of the most important prayers on *Rosh HaShana* and *Yom Kippur* relates: God is the sound of a still soft voice. In the book of *Kings*, Elijah flees to the wilderness, to hide in a cave. Perhaps this cave is connected to the cave where Koby was killed. There, Elijah was told that God would appear. He felt a strong wind, heard an earthquake, and saw a fire, but God was not in any of these. God instead was in a soft hushed sound. God's presence is not something that forces you to recognize it; you have to listen very hard to hear. You have to make room for it in your own silence. That's the silence in this canyon: it's not an emptiness. The silence is like putting your ear to the hush of a shell that has been waiting for you to pick it up from the beginning of time.

The silence of the cave, the silence of the canyon—in the face of pain and suffering, silence respects the mystery of life and the limits of language. It says that there is more to our lives than we can speak about. It admits there is another way of knowing and that knowing is sometimes in the space between words.

Silence can be holy. In the Torah reading for the Sabbath before Koby was killed, when Aaron, the High Priest, learned that his two sons had been killed after they brought a strange fire into the Holy Sanctuary where they were forbidden to go, Moses consoled him by telling him that the two boys were greater than they. Moses told Aaron that God said he would sanctify himself through those close to Him in order to be honored by the entire nation. It is a difficult consolation, painful. Yet Aaron answered with silence. As a result of his silence, Aaron was rewarded by having God speak to him, alone (not through Moses). God's speech, though, told Aaron that the High Priest was forbidden from drinking wine before entering the temple. The Abarbanel, a fifteenth century Spanish Biblical commentator, philosopher, and finance minister understands this commandment to mean that it may be that if you are silent in the moment of your grief and don't express your sorrow, you may turn to liquor to cover up the pain that wasn't expressed. For the High Priest, so close to God, and a model for the people, silence was the necessary response to his pain. But very few people can answer suffering with silence. And as the Abarbanel tells us, there is danger in being too stoic. There is no one prescription for grieving. In London, when I meet Lady Jacobovich, a Holocaust survivor and the wife of the former Chief Rabbi of England, she tells me: "We're all alone with God and all we have is our faith. What can I say to you—except stand with you in silence." Perhaps God is in a still hushed voice because it is silence that respects mystery.

❧

The wadi drew them down. Koby told a friend that he wanted to know the wadi like the back of his hand. The two boys were both newcomers to our village. All the other boys knew the wadi, which is rich with not just nature, but history, a favorite hiding place for rebels. Jonathan, the youngest Maccabee son, encamped here in 160 BC to take refuge and build up strength for the continuing fight against the Syrians. King Herod built his palace and fortress about a mile away from here, around the year of 25 BC. In the first revolt, before the destruction of the Second Temple, a Jewish zealot, Bar Giora, camped at Tekoa while he and his followers fought against the Romans. More than sixty years later, one of Bar Kochba's garrisons was stationed here. Bar Kochba, who rebelled against the Romans, was regarded by many, including Rabbi Akiva, the leading sage of his generation, as the Messiah. In the Talmud, it is stated: Rabbi Shimon Bar Yochai said: "Rabbi Akiva, my teacher, expounded the passage 'There shall go forth a star out of Jacob (Numbers 24:17).'" In this interpretation, Bar Kochba (the name is connected to the Hebrew word for star) might be seen as the fruition of the blessing that God made to Jacob after his dream of the ladder. The blessing stated that God would give Jacob the land of Israel, and his people would spread across the land, and through him, all of the families on the earth would be blessed. Yet, although initially successful in fighting the Romans, Bar Kochba could not save the Jews.*

During the Bar Kochba rebellion, a letter was sent to Tekoa because some of the wealthier residents were disregarding their mobilization orders and refusing to fight. In the letter, Bar Kochba admonished the people of Tekoa for not joining in the struggle against the Romans, telling them they would be punished for not fighting.

---

* Rabbi Akiva was cruelly tortured by the Romans and died sanctifying God's name.

61

But history was not what drew the boys down to the wadi that day. Koby's friends told me that the boys were heading through the rugged canyons toward the spring that surges out of the dry desert landscape. One of the marvels of a spring is that it doesn't overflow but is always in a perfect balance between giving and receiving. And it keeps replenishing itself, without overflowing its borders. It is a source of life, of unending life, of renewal. You can take all you want from a spring and it still has more to give. It is like a nursing mother—the more the child nurses, the more milk the mother produces. Sometimes, the more we ask for, the more we receive. The spring is a symbol of abundance—take as much as you want: I will not be depleted.

But Koby and Yosef never made it to the spring. I don't yet know exactly what happened. They may have seen a group of Palestinian men chasing them. Perhaps my son ran into the cave to hide. He died there mangled, bloody, mutilated, with his blood painted on the walls of the cave.

In Hebrew, the roots of the words for blessing and pool of water are related. Blessing is like a flowing body of water between God and the recipient of his blessing. I have to remember that in the midst of the parched desert Koby and Yosef were on their way to a spring, a source of abundant life, and that in the vast landscape of pain, there is also a pool of blessing, waiting for me and my family—as the woman in the *shiva* told me. I don't feel it now, but I pray that I will find it.

The Memorial Tent

Chapter twelve

Entering the Sabbath

Koby died on Tuesday, and was buried on Wednesday night. There were two days of mourning before *Shabbat*. I knew that it was forbidden to mourn and be sad on *Shabbat* from the well-known account in the *midrash* (stories and homilies that are part of the Oral tradition) on Proverbs 31:10, concerning Bruriah, a renowned female Torah scholar, one of the only women mentioned in the Talmud whose legal opinions had great standing. Bruriah went to check on her two sick sons on the Sabbath and found them both dead. She covered them with a linen cloth. When her husband returned from synagogue for the dinner meal, she did not inform him of the children's death, so as not to disturb the sanctity of *Shabbat*. Instead, she told him that the boys were at the house of study. As soon as *Shabbat* was over, she asked her husband a question: "Early today a man came here and gave me something to keep for him, but now he has returned to ask for it back. Shall we return it or not?"

"He who has received something on deposit must surely return it to its owner," answered her husband.

"The sons entrusted to us for safekeeping have been returned to their owner," said Bruriah. "Our sons have returned to God."

I am not as equanimous as Bruriah. I'm sure she suffered too. But I don't know how I will put aside my pain for the coming Sabbath. The pain is too raw, too overwhelming, yet in a strange way, I need it. I want it. It is my connection with my dead son. *Shabbat* seems now to me to be a slap in the face—a day of tranquility and harmony, a day that is like a door giving us a crack into the light of the World-to-Come, when the world will be in peace. How can I find peace when my son lies dead in the grave? Two days earlier he was kissing me goodnight, telling me how much he loved me.

But Ruthie Gillis comes to guide me. I haven't met her before but I know her story. Her husband, Shmuel Gillis, a hematologist at Hadassah Hospital in Jerusalem, was a much loved doctor who worked with cancer patients, many of them Arabs. On his way home from the hospital three months earlier, he was murdered by terrorists in a drive-by shooting. She holds my hand and says: "God has a plan and we don't know what that plan is. But that's the way it is. You will go on."

She says her husband's funeral was on Friday and she and her five children and her parents and her community had to return from the cemetery and enter *Shabbat*. She tells me, "The *Shabbat* after Shmuel was killed was the highest *Shabbat* of our lives—people I loved were around me and there was singing and beauty and there was life. There was strength. There was love."

She sits and holds my hand. I think she is crazy. I think she is nothing like me. After she leaves, I wonder how I will even stay alive for the impending Sabbath. But I begin to get ready. During *shiva* one is not permitted to bathe. But in honor of *Shabbat*, I can bathe. During the *shiva* I have stayed indoors or in my yard according to Jewish law, but on *Shabbat*, it is permitted to leave the confines of one's home.

My older sister, Nancy, a writer and a lawyer, will arrive from America right before sunset. I am afraid to see her, afraid she will blame me for bringing Koby here in the first place. Somebody from the American embassy is picking her up. My friend Avraham Litzman has taken care of the travel plans.

When my sister arrives, I hold her and we cry. Koby seems more dead, because she loved him so. The last time she was here, we were celebrating Koby's *Bar Mitzvah*. Nancy and Koby are similar, both first born, both family historians, both able to remember most details. Being with her makes me miss him even more. I would like my sister Loren to come, but she has never been here. Ten months younger than me, she and I have chosen totally different lives. She lives on Long Island, ten miles from where we grew up. She is a great mother, volunteers in her children's school, and is married to a police sergeant. I think she is afraid to fly, afraid to come here. My mother has taken ill but is expected to join us later in the week.

It is time to light *Shabbat* candles. We walk to the memorial tent that is set up close to my house for Koby and Yosef. Friday night prayers will be held there. My heart quakes when I realize that the tent is on the same field where we celebrated Koby's *Bar Mitzvah,* eleven months earlier. The tent is decorated with candles and the boys' photographs and posters with kids' messages to them. There is a verse from Psalm 77—verse 16—written on a poster—the only verse that has both boys' names in it—"With your powerful arm, you redeemed your people, the sons of Jacob and Joseph."

The psalmist calls out to God not to forsake him in his pain, in his long and bitter exile. He understands that God is leading us, and that though God's footsteps are disguised, he does provide guidance for his nation, through his leaders, the sons of Jacob and Joseph.

In Hebrew, letters are also used as numerals, and in the psalms each prayer is accompanied by the corresponding Hebrew letters. Seventy-seven is '*oz*' which means strength. The numerical equivalent of the verse is *tet zayyin*, sixteen, the Hebrew day of the month of Iyar that the boys' bodies were found.

I see my car and it looks like a relic from another lifetime. I can't believe that life is still going on. People are talking, laughing.

The world should have stopped. But it hasn't. I'm not in this world though. I have traveled to the world of truth. It is as if a veil has been lifted and I can understand the language of the soul.

The sun is just starting to set. The air is slightly cool. I step slowly, as if I have just learned to walk. I hear people speaking: "That door is hard to open."

"The light is fading; it's almost sunset."

"It's time to light the candles."

"Did you lock the door?"

"Turn the lights off."

"Look at how that jewel sparkles."

The words explode in my brain like keys to another universe: words resonating through the worlds. They remind me that I don't understand anything. The candle is the soul. The jewel is the soul. The door has been locked but inside there is a candle burning. The soul cannot be extinguished.

When we return for the meal, the table is set beautifully—bouquets of flowers, homemade bread that neighbors have brought over for the Sabbath. Friends are there to sleep over and kids come to help serve us the food which has been made by neighbors. We sit down: Charlotte, originally from Queens, who lost her twin sister to cancer this year. Rachel, who once babysat for Koby, tells us how Koby tied her up that night, but how she got out by tickling him. Racheli, sixteen years old, who has a sister who is six foot seven, a star basketball player being recruited by American colleges. But her sister has been unable to play this year—she is recovering from a cancerous tumor that was removed from her hand.

There are balloons on the napkins and Charlotte says, "Those balloons remind me of Wonder bread."

"Wonder bread, what's that?" my children ask.

"You don't know what Wonder bread is?"

"That's what we need," says Nancy. "Wonder!"

And then we began to laugh about our Wonder bread childhoods, so far from this dinner table, and Racheli tells us she has a job at a 'Roman' restaurant in the Old City. Her job is fanning the guests with palm fronds, and she describes her uniform and her fanning technique. We try to think of the word for the occupation of professional fanner and I think: I can laugh. I can laugh and be silly. And I know that Koby would love this conversation—he so enjoyed the absurd—and I want to share it with him, the freedom of joy in our jokes, in our laughter, laughter that takes us up to another world.

We laugh and we sing, and neighbors come in to sing. The whole living room is filled with teenagers and friends singing. I know that at the bottom of the joy there is pain there, waiting for me. In a few hours, I will be lying on Koby's floor, weeping, being held by my daughter. I will look at his walls, the cartoons he tore out of the *New Yorker*, the pictures of Cal Ripken and Michael Jordan. I will feel like I want to die. But for a few hours, the Sabbath offers me the belief in peace, the belief in a respite from suffering.

Chapter thirteen

Levels of Pain

Some people tell me to be strong. They want me to reassure them that there is hope in the world. Keep going so that we can see that life is possible after your child is dead.

But what they mean by being strong is not what I mean. I believe that being strong means feeling pain, letting my body mourn, letting my mind mourn, letting my soul mourn—entering the pain, not fleeing it. Rabbi Adin Steinsaltz, the eminent Torah scholar, comes to see us and tells us that he also cut school as a kid, that he remembers a bomb exploding in the street when he was a little boy in Israel. He tells us there is no place in the soul for the loss of a child. "At first there will be people around you but eventually, they all go away. And then you are all alone and it's you and your pain." He does not distract us from the stark truth of our suffering—the pain will remain and it's up to us to find a way to live with it.

Pain is a rock you throw into a calm pond. It keeps expanding. As soon as you deal with one pain, there is another to take its place. There is the acute pain, which comes like a butcher knife to your heart; the pain when you see your son in a photograph, his sweet smile and wide-open eyes, so full of love and life. There is the chronic pain, the pain of missing him coming in the door, throwing his bag on the couch, bugging you for more to eat—the pain of knowing he will not return, that follows you like a dog biting your heels, so there is no such thing as peace. There is the pain of him not being there for his siblings—their big brother—not there to pick them up and twirl them around, not there to play basketball with them, not there to show off his juggling—like a sledge hammer pounding the back of your head. Then there is the pain of losing your future with him, his future, and your own, somehow tied together. The oldest son, I imagined him as a lawyer or a judge, with a future of power and strength, and somehow those were my power and strength. Now I will never see his graduation, his choice of wife, his children, his choice of career—how his face would have turned into a man's face. There is the pain which is a vise around your throat of not talking to him—the pain of losing a shared sensibility. And then there is the pain of the cruelty inflicted upon him. That pain threatens to swallow you, like a python that will eat you whole. And then there is the pain of knowing that you are still not immune, God forbid, you and your other children. The pain of knowing that death is there lurking in the corner for all of you. That pain is a tiger that growls in your sleep and wakes you with sharp teeth, snarling, ready to maul you. There is the pain of seeing his friends and knowing—they are alive and your lovely, beautiful, brilliant son is dead. That pain is a desert you cross for days without water or food. That is the pain you're in today.

Today he would have graduated junior high school. They will show a video of his friends speaking about him. A friend casually says how she doesn't want to go to her son's graduation from junior high because it will be boring. The pain of hearing that is like nails scraping against concrete.

In ten years, you will be the only one still thinking every day about your son. To go on you need to let the pain mark you like the years are marked inside the trunk of a tree. Even as you mark each day of missing him, you need to find a way to be enlarged by it.

Chapter fourteen

The Bullet and
the Jewelry Box

I really don't know what God was thinking, but I am sure of one thing: he had a message to send me that night.

As a teacher of writing, I know there are many ways of emphasizing a point, for example, underlining the text, using repetition, putting in lots of exclamation points!!!!!, as well as WRITING IN CAPITAL LETTERS. I used to tell my students that it was a mistake to employ too many modes of emphasis, because if you emphasized too much, then you emphasized nothing. But God did not take my class. God used all—a whole array of techniques—the night of the shooting. And still I didn't see the message until later. Until after we were at the hotel.

It happened on the evening of May 21st. Seth was driving my sister and mother to Ben Gurion airport for their flight back to New York after the *shiva*. I was home with the kids. There was a ceremony at the synagogue because it was Jerusalem Day, a holiday when we celebrate the city's unification in 1967. On this day, the Israeli army liberated the Western Wall and East Jerusalem from Jordanian control. Rabbi Eliyahu Bakshi Doron, the chief Sephardic rabbi, was speaking at the synagogue in Tekoa. I wasn't planning to go. I didn't want to leave my house. I didn't want to be part of a group of people. But my friend, Hadera, came over to convince me to join her. The rabbi was already speaking when we arrived. He was wearing a black brocaded gown and a skull cap that looked like a jaunty fez and as he spoke I could hear Koby in my head: "Take a look at this guy's get-up. Who does he think he is?" I could hear him laughing and I cracked a smile. Maybe he was with me, I thought. My daughter, Eliana, sat next to me and as soon as the lecture was finished I started on my way home. Rena Ish-Ran, Yosef's mother, called out to me and told me that the rabbi wanted to bless us. Eliana ran ahead home and I continued on to a small classroom in the synagogue. There was Bakshi Doron.

He blessed me, speaking quickly in Hebrew that I didn't understand. Then he wished me comfort to face the difficult days ahead. I started home. My house is a minute's walk from the synagogue and as I made my way home, Eliana and her friend came flying out of my house, screaming.

"There was an explosion," Eliana said, crying. Confused, I put my arms around her. "What happened?" I asked. "Tell me what happened."

"I don't know," she said. "I was sitting downstairs and all of a sudden I saw a flash of light, and there was this huge noise."

The boys from Koby's class spilled out onto the path in front of my home. They had heard the explosion and come running to our house and up the stairs to Eliana's room to check what had happened. I ran upstairs. The window in Eliana's room was shattered. Nobody knew what had caused it. Broken glass from the window was scattered on the floor, right next to Eliana's desk. On the floor was her jewelry box, burned, scorched black with a hole gashed through the middle. On the desk was a bottle of colored sand I had collected in the Painted Canyon in the Sinai Desert in Egypt. The bottle was scored with a black burn mark. The shimmering pale gray hexagonal crystal rock that the boys had found while digging Koby's grave was there too, untouched.

My friend Shira ran upstairs with me. In America, Shira had studied with Elizabeth Kubler-Ross and was a pastoral counselor in hospitals, working with the families of sick and dying people. After Koby's death, Shira's daily visits helped me to absorb the great pain I was suffering.

But now there was more trauma to process. I saw a bottle of nail polish remover on the floor, empty. Searching for an explanation that would satisfy me without terrifying me, I said, "It's the nail polish remover. It exploded," I said.

"How?" asked Shira. "How could it explode and break the window?"

"I don't know. Don't they say not to put it near a flame? Maybe it got hot somehow. Maybe it was too close to the light. How do I know?" I paused. "It's possible, right?"

Shira looked at me and shook her head. "It doesn't sound right."

"Okay, then it's Koby," I said to Shira. "He came back. He's a poltergeist." I was relieved, happy. He had returned to us, causing trouble like always.

"Could be," said Shira. "It's like Koby. Powerful. Strong. Unpredictable."

People came running from their houses, upstairs to Eliana's room. A few minutes later, Yisrael, a husky man in charge of security in our village walked in. Yisrael is a black belt in karate and he measures his words before he speaks. With his strength and his quiet demeanor, he is a reassuring presence. He explained that for the first time, Palestinians had fired on our village, from a mile away—a Hail Mary bullet, without much chance of finding a target. One other house had a bullet through an outside wall. After Yisrael left, other security men came running up the stairs. They didn't see any bullet holes but surmised that a bullet had entered one side of my daughter's room and exited the other side, via the window.

My friend Harvey, a big strapping six-foot guy from New Jersey, joined us and located the bullet hole. It was near my daughter's closet, about the size of a half dollar.

I went downstairs with my kids and my friends. Two houses had been hit. I didn't understand why ours was one of them. We, after all, lived in the middle of the village. It made no sense that our house had been hit and not a house on the periphery.

I could feel myself begin to quake inside. I called my husband on his cellphone and explained that he should tell my mother and sister that I was sick and that he had to return home immediately. I didn't want to scare them and tell them about the bullet.

I looked at Eliana's jewelry box. It was pink cardboard with a pattern of flowers and stars. Laced around the edge of the jewelry box, the designer had written this over and over: Good things happen when you believe in yourself.

It was precisely that belief which had been blasted from our world. I had believed in myself. I had also believed that God and the world would protect me. And believing hadn't been enough.

The ballerina had been blasted off of her pedestal. All of the jewelry had been destroyed. Except for one piece. A pendant for a necklace. Inside was a tightly wrapped scroll—the traveler's prayer, a prayer we say before driving or going on a trip. "May you God lead us toward peace and make us reach our desired destination for peace. May you rescue us from the hand of every foe and ambush along the way..."

Peace was a long way away, both peace inside of me, for my family, and peace for the nation. My friends stayed with me, comforting me, bringing me tea. I was relieved when my husband returned from the airport. We pulled mattresses into the living room and all slept there, since the walls are thickest there, the most protected area in the house.

Seth and I woke up very early. We needed to get out of the house, out of Tekoa. We felt that the house was cursed. Even the neighborhood. And we were paying the price. We remembered that our next door neighbor had recently had a string of bad luck: her nine-year-old son had been bitten by a scorpion in the middle of the night; he had also had his bare foot gashed by a blade when changing his skates at a skating rink nearby. Both times he had been rushed to the emergency room. Both times, thank God, he'd recovered quickly.

Seth said that sometimes the Angel of Death was out, unleashed, and that especially for the first year after a family member's death, it was important to take special care. We decided to go into Jerusalem and stay in a hotel for a while, until we could decide what to do next.

We packed up some clothes and books and took a taxi to the hotel in Jerusalem. We were too afraid to drive ourselves. As we drove the tunnel road into Jerusalem, there was shooting from Bethlehem. I was terrified and thought: Please, don't let us get hurt. Please, just keep us alive. The driver continued onward, as if nothing unusual was happening.

At the hotel, we put the kids in one room; we were in an adjoining room. They put on their TV, we put on ours and we tried to relax, to calm down for a minute. But we could not forget that we had just had a son killed and a bullet had gone through our daughter's room.

I could only thank God that she was okay.

While we are away, our friends take the scrolls from inside the *mezuzahs* affixed to each doorway in our home, and from Seth's and Koby's prayer phylacteries and bring them to be checked. On the scrolls of the mezuzah and phylacteries are inscribed the biblical passage, the *Shema*—"Hear O Israel. The Lord our God. God is one." Inside the phylacteries are some other biblical passages. The letters need to be written perfectly. Sometimes if a letter is erased or misshapen, it can be linked to some traumatic event in a person's life. But it turned out that all of our phylacteries, *mezuzahs*, as well as our wedding contract were perfectly written.

Bad luck? Faulty scribe work? The wrong neighborhood? Our own sins? No, nothing we could have possibly done could have visited such wrath upon us. We couldn't blame anybody or anything. But all week, in the midst of visits from friends bringing us treats and toys and books; and informal meetings with reporters from NBC News and the *Jerusalem Report*, I worried. I felt that the meaning of the destroyed jewelry box could help me in some way, but I didn't know how. Its meaning nagged at me, like an untied shoelace. Later in the week, my friend Valerie visited and told me that my neighbor's house across the street had also been shot at. Zvi and Noga and their five kids had been away on vacation for the week and had returned to find that their daughter's room had been shot at. A bullet had sliced through the wall. And what had been damaged? Their young daughters' jewelry box, a hole smack through it and everything inside of it, cheap costume jewelry, destroyed. It seemed incredible that two different, random, bullets could both find the same target—a little girl's jewelry box. Valerie went into the room where Eliana was watching TV. She asked Eliana about the pendant that had been untouched by the bullet, the one with the traveler's prayer rolled up inside. Eliana told her that she had bought the pendant just a month earlier, on a school trip up north, at the grave of Shimon bar Yochai.

I'd totally forgotten about her trip up north. As soon as Valerie told me, I got the message. Shimon Bar Yochai, who had entered the cave, who had left the real world, was telling me—the box had been destroyed. The box was burned, torn, ruined. The outside, the covering, was gone. But a jewel remained. Not cheap costume jewelry. But a real jewel. The jewel of my son's soul. That could not be diminished, tarnished, destroyed. That was still shining. That was still alive, and that was still speaking to us.

The fact that the jewel that remained whole in Eliana's jewelry box contained the traveler's prayer told me that this world is a world of transition, of sojourn, a world where we are all temporary travelers—and we're all heading toward one destination. After death, we have a place waiting for us, nearer or further from God, depending on our actions in this world.

Koby's death gives me the comfort of knowing that when I

reach my final destination there will be someone I have thought of every day, longed for every day, waiting to see me. Koby's death makes me see my eventual death as a reunion with my son, a return to the unblemished purity of the jewel of my soul.

Chapter fifteen

The Shooting Star

I n order to heal you have to look outside of yourself, you have to look up. But it's not easy when you're drenched in grief. We looked up the night of Mr. Tobin's funeral. He is buried in the same place as Koby, the Kfar Etzion cemetery. Also buried there are the fighters from 1948 who lived on Kibbutz Kfar Etzion. After the State of Israel was declared, the Arabs began to fight against the fledgling state. The women and children of Kfar Etzion were sent to Jerusalem. When the Jewish fighters ran out of ammunition, they fought the Arabs off hand to hand. Nearly every Jewish fighter was killed. The children of the original founders live on the kibbutz today; one of them, Tuli, is the city manager of Tekoa. Some of them were at Koby's funeral.

Mr. Tobin's son, Michael, a psychologist, is a friend who later became my employer at a family website he created with Toby Green-wald: *wholefamily.com.*

Mordechai Tobin died at the age of eighty-six in his home in Efrat. In the 1980s, when his son Michael became religious and moved to Jerusalem, Mr. Tobin traveled to Jerusalem to convince him to return to America. Instead, Mr. Tobin became interested in religion and returned to Israel. In his sixties, he remarried and began to learn the Talmud. His goal was to learn the entire Talmud. He was still studying strong almost to the day he died.

When Mr. Tobin was dying of cancer in his home, I visited him a few times with my children. My father had died of cancer in Florida the previous year, six months after we moved to Israel. He was diagnosed and three months later, he was dead. I think I was drawn to visit Mr. Tobin because my children hadn't seen my father sick or gone to the funeral. Taking them to Mr. Tobin's satisfied an urge in me to tend a dying man together with my family; to try to bring him some happiness, some light.

When Mr. Tobin died, Seth and I took Gavi and Eliana to the funeral. Driving home from Mr. Tobin's funeral at the Kfar Etzion cemetery, we admired the stars. The night was crisp and clear, and you could see the Seven Sisters and the Big Dipper. And then, all at once, we saw two shooting stars one after the other. They swooshed across the sky.

"Looks like God is welcoming Mr. Tobin," I said.

Seeing those stars prepared for the message God sent me almost two years later, thirty days after Koby's murder.

The period for mourning a parent is a year. For a year, the child cannot attend weddings or *Bar Mitzvah*s, listen to live music, or buy new clothes. The mourner is supposed to refrain from anything too celebratory, so as not to detract from the respect and honor due to a parent after death.

I was surprised when I found out that the halachic, traditional Jewish period for mourning a child is only thirty days. But one of the mothers explained why: it's because you grieve the rest of your life. You don't need the rituals to remind you to grieve. You will think of your child forever. Any new piece of clothing you buy will remind you that you can no longer take him shopping; you will not want to go to a party and dance; you will not want to sing and listen to music; you will want to stay home and grieve and honor his memory. But Jewish law encourages you to live, to go on.

To mark the thirtieth day of Koby and Yosef's death, the

shloshim, the end of the mourning period, our village devotes an entire day to remembering the boys. Everyone in the village receives a special memorial candle to burn all day. The candle has the verse from Psalm 77—Koby and Yosef's verse—written on it: "With your powerful arm, you redeemed your people, the sons of Jacob and Joseph."

A "fast of speech" is also declared for the day. That doesn't mean that we don't speak. It means that for that day we speak well of each other and ourselves: no negative language, no name-calling, and no gossip. We replace words that hurt with words that encourage.

It is also a fast day if people decide to join in. It is a day of classes, of art workshops, of learning, of prayer. In the evening I go to the synagogue for the special prayer service in memory of the boys. Seth speaks about how Koby is no longer alive to serve God and do good, so now everybody has to do more, do something extra to make up for what was lost in the world.

I pray and cry: "Please God give me a sign. Please show me that he is okay. I need to know that he is okay."

My friends have prepared a meal in the synagogue to break the fast. Everyone stands around eating, talking, even laughing. I don't want to stay where people are finished with mourning. Where people feel a sense of accomplishment; where they feel good. I know I have a long dark path in front of me.

I walk out alone in the darkness to go home. The air is cool and fresh and the night is black. Something draws me to look up. And the minute I look up, I see a shooting star sweep across the sky. The same shooting star that Gavi told me Koby would be able to see now, because he was with God. A shooting star like the ones I saw after Mr. Tobin's funeral.

God is welcoming Koby.

Chapter sixteen

Koby's Birthday— Becoming Holy Beggars

June 14th should have been Koby's fourteenth birthday. Instead, he's been dead for five weeks. It feels like he's been dead for five hours. The pain is so raw. But it is his birthday, and Shira, my friend and guide in grieving, has told me I must do something to mark Koby's birthday.

We go into Jerusalem because we need to renew our passports. Seeing Koby's passport as I rifle through our official documents makes me want to grab his passport and renew it. Instead it is as if he will be erased. I cry in the passport office.

The kids and I decide to go to Burger King to honor Koby's birthday because one thing Koby loved about Israel was being able to eat kosher hamburgers. Koby loved to eat—but particularly hamburgers. Even on the screensaver on our computer, he wrote: "I'm hungry, give me something to eat now!!!" His hunger was a force to be reckoned with, a being in itself.

We have to walk about five blocks to get to Burger King. We're hungry and tired and cranky so when we pass a vegetarian restaurant—we decide to stop there to eat. I think we are all relieved not to have to feel the sadness of eating hamburgers without Koby.

My kids go to pick up the drinks at the counter of the restaurant, and I close my eyes and hold a napkin against my eyes as I cry and I wonder: how am I going to go on? How am I going to stand up? How am I going to get the strength to leave this restaurant and take my children home on the bus?

And suddenly I think: On my birthday I like to swim a mile. What am I going to do on Koby's birthday? Swim fourteen laps? We're in downtown Jerusalem; Koby would have been fourteen. When my kids return to the table, I say to my kids: "Let's go give charity to fourteen beggars in Koby's name."

At that instant, a gentleman with a clean-shaven face and puffy white hair places a card on our table. With a glance, I know that the card says that the man is deaf and looking for a contribution.

In the past cards like that annoyed me—I was trying to eat a meal in peace, and suddenly some beggar had interrupted me. Now I and my kids are thrilled to see him. "Here," we say, "here's money." He looks at us with a grin on his face.

We get change and exit the restaurant, energized by our mission. But it's hot and there aren't many people downtown because of the fear of terrorism. We see a man giving charity to an old stooped man. The old man walks away and we run after him to give him money. We stride up to two people who have broken legs and are resting on a bench because we think they're beggars and are disappointed that there's no cup or change basket.

Up in heaven, I think, Koby is laughing at our escapades. There is nothing he loved more than irony and this is supreme irony: we need beggars because we are desperate for someone to give to. We are begging for beggars. And just when we need them, there aren't any. Perhaps this is Koby's message to us: his spirit is alive and connected to us.

It's too hot to stay out much longer though. We think about visiting the Western Wall, where there is usually a good group of beggars, but it's the middle of the afternoon and it's too hot to be out more. So we decide that next year on Koby's birthday, we will get up early, go to the Western Wall, and make sure to give away money to fifteen beggars in Koby's name.

When I later tell my husband about the fourteen beggars, he says, "Next year, we'll gather the beggars and take them out to a restaurant for a meal."

I know that Koby would think it was cool to sit with the beggars at a table. We have become holy beggars, like the ones in a story told by Shlomo Carlebach, a rabbi who died in 1994, and in his lifetime brought many people closer to Judaism with his heartfelt songs, learning and generosity. Koby has made us holy beggars, people who are begging to give, begging to create love. That is his gift to us.

Koby's Bar Mitzvah

Chapter seventeen

The *Bar Mitzvah*

Koby was killed the year of his *Bar Mitzvah*. I am glad he got to celebrate taking on the commandments. There had been no *Bar Mitzvah*s in my family for three generations. My father, an only child, didn't have one because his birthday was in the summer and they were up in a bungalow colony and decided not to celebrate it. Neither my mother nor her sister were given a religious upbringing, so there were no religious celebrations in her family either. I am one of three sisters and none of us had a *Bat Mitzvah* or even a confirmation. So Koby's *Bar Mitzvah* was a breakthrough event for us.

Preparing for Koby's *Bar Mitzvah* was an education in itself. One of my friends said to me: a *Bar Mitzvah* is not only a sign that your son is growing up, but a sign that you are growing up as well.

Koby was definitely growing up. I let him make all of the major decisions about his *Bar Mitzvah*. He decided where it would be held (a field near our house overlooking the wadi), and what would be served (our friend Shimon's fried chicken). He picked out his own invitations, blue on white, and he wrote the wording and picked out the quotation he wanted on his invitation. *"And God chose Jacob for his own, Israel as his treasure."*

At first when Koby began to study his *Bar Mitzvah* bible portion, *Chukat*, Numbers 19–22, with a teacher, the teacher called us and said he didn't think Koby would be able to learn the whole reading. But Koby persisted. The Torah has to be recited perfectly to ensure the transmission of the tradition. If you make a mistake, you are corrected, sometimes loudly and vociferously. Koby was embarrassed about his accent and worried about how he would sound. But on the day of his *Bar Mitzvah*, Koby didn't need any corrections.

We had a party on Thursday night, and on Saturday morning, we had a hundred people for kiddush, fifty people for each of the Sabbath meals. Friday night I watched Koby dancing on the men's side of the synagogue, his face shining, looking up. Later, when I asked Koby what his favorite part of the *Bar Mitzvah* had been, he said, the Torah reading. When he said that, I felt gratified. All the sacrifices we had made to move back to Israel were worth it—our difficult financial situation, our troubles finding jobs, the problems our kids had faced coming to Israel without speaking Hebrew. Koby understood the beauty of being a Jew; it was a natural, organic part of him, it was an expression of his deepest essence.

Chukat, or "statute", the portion of the Torah that Koby read in synagogue, is one that helps me now to deal with the pain of Koby's death. *Chukot* are statutes that we keep because God commanded them; the meaning of why we do them is not clear to us. Some commandments seem logical to us (for example don't steal, have a system of courts, don't commit adultery) but there are those which don't seem logical even though they are divinely ordained (for example, keeping kosher, putting on *tefillin*, prohibiting the use of linen and wool in the same garment).

The Torah portion opens with the burning of the red heifer, the prototype of inexplicable statutes in the Torah. A perfect red heifer is chosen and burned by the priest so that those who have come into contact with a corpse can be purified. The ashes of the red heifer are mixed with spring water and then the priest sprinkles this mixture on those who need to be purified. Fire and water, two opposites, join to purify. But the ashes can also contaminate. The priest who concocts the potions of the red heifer becomes impure. The priest must wash his clothes and his body after burning the red heifer.

The goal is holiness; with each purification comes further contamination. The two are intimately wed. The cycle is unending, infinite. Some Torah commentators say that the red heifer is a tikkun, a healing that comes to rectify the sin of the golden calf, the idol that the Jews built when Moses went to receive the Torah from God, and after forty days, returned back late to the camp. The people, in their fear and frustration, built an idol from gold. The red heifer atones for the idol worship of the people. Only the heifer, the mother, can truly ask for forgiveness for her child, the golden calf. Rashi says, "Let the mother come and clean up the mess made by her child."

It is a mother's role to clean up the mess, like it or not. But Koby's death is a tragedy, not a mess. I must be careful not to turn Koby's death into a form of idol worship. I must not let my mind and spirit be consumed by murder. And so I must work on accepting what God has given me. And the law of the red heifer teaches me to believe in God—and accept His will—even though I will never understand Him. The statutes tell us that it is not our job to understand everything. We can't think that we can penetrate everything with our reason and intellect. Some things are beyond the limits of our language.

Precisely because it is beyond our understanding, the law of the red heifer enters the world of paradox: the same substance can purify or contaminate depending on the circumstances. The same substance can be holy or profane, depending on how we use it.

Chukot tell us that we need to live with contradiction, need to live with things unexplained; need to do things just because God commands it, God desires it. And Koby's death seems to say the same thing. I have to live with the contradiction of my son's death—the suffering I experience in the midst of an outpouring of love and support; a son who is alive in my mind and dead at the same time; my need to live in this world and reach towards the World-to-Come, the terrible beauty of the place that he was killed. Only God, in the words of scholar Avivah Zornberg "contains and harmonizes contraries within himself." God is the one who can untangle contradiction. We on this earth can't engage in both sides of a dialectic. Rabbi Shlomo Carlebach said that our minds can only be one thing, happy or sad. But our souls are both. "The soul is crying and laughing at the same time...the soul is one...Sometimes you meet people and they touch this oneness in your soul. Then it is both crying and laughing, utmost sadness and utmost joy," says Shlomo.

Now I long for people who can touch the oneness in my soul. People who don't pity me. People who can speak of sadness and know that at the same time, joy dwells within me, waiting to be discovered.

Koby's death is like one of the *chukot*, a statute that I can't understand. Yet, I need to believe that his death is leading us some-where, and that place, though a place of paradox and contradiction, is also filled with holiness.

Chapter eighteen

The Cricket

Even insects can be messengers. Six weeks after the murder, I come downstairs first thing in the morning, heavy with longing for Koby. Sleep doesn't refresh me but only makes me want my son more. Because it is morning, it is a new day, and Koby is not here to help me welcome it.

I put the kettle on and all of a sudden there is a cricket making a racket. He sounds like bells from a sleigh, a magical chime cutting through the frigid snow of loss, a sound that says—*I'm here! I won't leave you alone.* The sound gets louder, calling out for attention. It is unremitting, jarring.

Every morning for over a month the cricket is there, waiting for me when I wake. I know that it is male crickets who chirp, and usually, only at night. They produce sound by rubbing their wings together, bringing the thickened vein of one wing into contact with the hard, sharp-edged portion of the other. But this cricket is making his racket during the day. This is what I crave—contact with Koby. I come down to the kitchen each morning heartsick, put on the kettle, and then I hear the cricket and feel somehow soothed. He is alive and he is chirping—sometimes loudly, sometimes in a soothing hum, and he will not be silenced. But in the summer, two months after Koby's murder, we travel to America and leave my cricket. I am afraid that the cricket will depart while we are gone. I am afraid of silence when I return home.

I'm right. The cricket is not there when we return. Okay, it was only a cricket I tell myself. No big deal. I want Koby, not a cricket. Still when I come downstairs in the morning, I am depressed. I miss my wake up call.

Two months later, I send the first chapters of this book to an agent. She calls me later that day, praising the book with superlatives. Perhaps I should explain that the whole time I've had children, I've been writing. I've written children's stories and novels, many essays, and while I've had many articles and a book published, I've never received accolades from an agent before, especially not an agent who represents leading writers.

Koby would sometimes praise my work; sometimes he laughed at it. He always had something to say about it. He was my most faithful reader. Sometimes he would go into my computer files and read my articles, just to see what I was up to. He was a wonderful audience.

The night that Deborah Harris calls, I am awakened in the middle of the night by a shrill, piercing sound. I assume one of my children has mistakenly set an alarm clock. I go downstairs in the dark house, into their rooms, looking for the alarm clock. I can't find it. My husband comes down, woken by the same racket. I say, "I think it's an alarm clock."

We search, but we can't find a clock. We want to go back to sleep but it's impossible unless we locate the source of the shrill sound. We move closer and closer to the sound. Seth calls me into the kitchen. "You're not going to believe it," he says.

The cricket is back, and with a vengeance. He's having a party, making a racket, having the time of his life. It's as if he's been crowned King of the Crickets and had his first CD released—with a movie tie-in—all on the same day. I take this as a sign that Koby is thrilled with news of the book. He wants me to know he's with me. But he knows, and I know too, that the good news of the book now has a reverse image. Just when I get the approval, the validation I sought for so long, it is laced with regret, for I have lost the one thing I need, the one thing I require for happiness.

Then I hear Nitzan's voice. Nitzan is a psychic out of central casting with her flowing white cotton dress, long black hair, and dark eyes that seem to see into the future. Nitzan came to us the week after Koby died. She sat in my bedroom and held my hand and told me, "Koby wants you to finish the project you began together."

Now I realize that our project is this book. He is with me, urging me forward, helping me to tell our story. Months later I tell the cricket story to a filmmaker from France. She looks at me and says: "Don't you know? In the south of France, they never kill a cricket. The cricket is a symbol of the soul."

Chapter nineteen

The Broken Glass

Carly is my friend Valerie's oldest daughter. Carly is going to marry Yehuda. She is eighteen and he is twenty. It's three months after Koby's death. I know I have to go to this wedding. But it is so hard to be in a place of joy when your heart and your soul ache. Still Seth and I and the kids attended Carly and Yehuda's wedding, and I cried because of the beauty of the wedding but also for myself. I will never have the glory of seeing Koby married. I will never be able to know the woman he would have chosen for his bride.

I cry and grieve, but at the same time, I have not shut down my capacity for feeling joy and awe at the world. On the contrary, it is as if my palate of emotion has expanded. Now when I feel joy it is more exquisite because I know that love needs to be held on to, gathered close, appreciated because it is so precious. Being home when my children return from school is a moment of gratitude for me.

My heart now feels like a heart of truth, a heart that yearns for eternity. It's a heart that is broken like the goblet at a Jewish wedding ceremony.

At my own wedding, I had learned the meaning of breaking

the glass. I knew that it meant that even in the greatest of happiness, we need to remember our obligations to God—not to get too carried away in our joy. It reminds us that we are always dependent on God's mercy. It reminds us that we can't have complete happiness because of the destruction of the Temple, the place of God's dwelling, in Jerusalem. It reminds us that perfect joy is not possible in this world.

Back then, I understood the meaning of the broken glass in an abstract way. Now I have lived the broken glass. God himself seeks out broken vessels for use (*Leviticus Rabah* 7:2). As it says in Psalm 147, verse 3, "God is the healer of shattered hearts." Now I understand that there is a shattering first. Then there will be a healing. It is out of destruction that the Resurrection will come. The Messiah was born on the day that the Temple was destroyed. It is out of pain that the Messiah will be born. In this world, pain and beauty coexist. In the World-to-Come, as I understand it, the pain will be gone. We won't need answers to our suffering, because we will no longer have questions.

In the book *Made in Heaven*, Aryeh Kaplan teaches us that a human being can be likened to glass—vulnerable. But glass, when it is broken, can be re-melted and re-blown. It can be made whole again. So, too, even after a person dies, his life is not over. He too can be restored, made whole. And so, too, can our hearts. Though I will never again be that same innocent bride, and I will never again look at a wedding without pain in my heart, I have become a different person, one who is more vulnerable, more open and, I hope, has more compassion. I pray that one day I will meet my son in the World-to-Come. All of the broken fragments of the world will be mended, and I will know that as Rabbi Menachem Mendel of Kotsk, a nineteenth century Chassidic rabbi, said: There is nothing so whole as a broken heart.

Chapter twenty

Shimon Bar Yochai

Ordinary life fills me with dread. I am in the changing room after swimming. It's about four months after Koby's death. Two women discuss their daughters' wardrobes. One says that she bought her daughter a skirt at Penny's when she was in America the previous summer; that it was half the price of buying one in Israel. The other woman discusses the prices of the shoes in the Land's End Catalogue. The women continue on, talking about whether they have half sizes for leather boots, and if they should buy boots with fur, because it's not a freezing cold winter here.

I resent them for having this conversation while I am in the room. I cannot share their interest in fabrics and sizes and prices. I have come here to swim to encourage the pain to move through me. I want to breathe so fast, work so hard, that the name Koby will not be a cymbal in my head for this half hour.

I remember the first night after the funeral. Some people came in and began to talk about their doctor, about his bedside manner, and I felt revolted that they were talking about something that had nothing to do with Koby. Suddenly, in the locker room, I understand

Rabbi Shimon Bar Yochai, who spent twelve years in a cave and then came out, unable to cope with the everyday world. These women have inspired hostility from deep within me, hostility that they can spend their time on trivial concerns, while people are suffering, are in pain; while others live with death on their shoulders.

The night before Koby was killed I went to a class and studied the story of Shimon Bar Yochai. It was the week of the holiday of *Lag b'Omer*. The two Hebrew letters, *lamed* and *gimel*, that make up the word 'Lag' form the numerical equivalent of thirty-three. This is the thirty-third day of the *Omer* period, the seven week period counted between Passover and Shavuot. Since Rabbi Shimon is said to have both come out from the cave, and later died on *Lag b'Omer*, the holiday honors him (as well as the students of Rabbi Akiva, who are said to have stopped dying from the plague on that day). Rabbi Shimon Bar Yochai was a student of Rabbi Akiva, a martyr who died praising God. It is said that on the day that Shimon Bar Yochai died, he taught his students the Torah's hidden lessons and the sun did not set until he had finished. Rabbi Shimon Bar Yochai wanted his death to be a day of celebration, not of mourning, a day of celebrating all of the Torah he had taught on that day.

Most people believe that Shimon Bar Yochai's grave is in the north of Israel, at Mount Meron, and thousands of people gather there on the night of *Lag b'Omer* and celebrate with bonfires to remember the light of wisdom that Shimon Bar Yochai brought into the world. But there are others who claim that his grave is in our wadi.

Shimon Bar Yochai and his son, Eliezer, went into the cave to hide from the Romans, who wanted to capture Rabbi Shimon for impugning the Roman government. While there, the two learned every day, revealing the secrets of the Torah, calling forth the hidden divine light of every letter in the holy books. It is said that the prophet, Elijah taught them there. It is widely believed that it was in this cave that Shimon Bar Yochai composed the *Zohar*, the primary book of Jewish mystical teachings (though there are scholars who attribute authorship of the *Zohar* to Moses de Leon, who lived at the end of the thirteenth century).

What did the two of them live on, other than words of Torah? While a cave can be a grave, it can also be a womb. For these two, it was a womb with nourishment. A carob tree grew to provide them with food, and a spring appeared to give them water. They took off their clothes to preserve them, only putting them on for prayers and for the Sabbath. During the day they covered themselves with sand so that they would not profane their learning. They buried themselves in a life of holiness.

After twelve years, Elijah came to the mouth of the cave and reported that the Roman emperor had died and the decree to execute Rabbi Shimon Bar Yochai and his son had been annulled. Now they could emerge from their concealment.

When Shimon Bar Yochai came out of the cave, he saw that the world was the same as when he had left. He saw people plowing a field, life going on as if nothing had changed. Shimon Bar Yochai glared at the people and his look was so piercing that whatever he looked at was reduced to ashes. Then a heavenly voice called out: "Have you come out of the cave to destroy my world? Return to your cave."

Rabbi Shimon and his son returned to the cave for another year. On a Friday, the two left the cave. When they came out, they saw an old man running, carrying two bundles of fresh myrtle branches. "Why are you carrying those?" they asked.

"To honor and remember the Sabbath," the old man replied.

This time, Rabbi Shimon and his son were able to reenter the world knowing that God's commandments were dear to the children of Israel.

Elie Wiesel likens Shimon Bar Yochai's tenuous emergence from the cave to the release of Holocaust prisoners after the war. When the survivors of concentration camps returned to life, they were confronted with the problem of what to do with their anger, their pain and their despair—what to do with the memories of feeling dead in life, of having their families slaughtered, their communities destroyed. Like Rabbi Shimon Bar Yochai, they could have destroyed creation. They could have murdered or become drug addicts or pillaged or committed arson. But they chose not to. The majority chose not to give in to despair. Many cried themselves to sleep every night, but they went on.

I will not surrender to despair or anger. Reporters ask me: "Aren't you angry?" Of course, I'm angry. But that is not where I put my energy. That's not what gets me up in the morning. To me, the murderers are brainwashed agents of evil, lacking humanity, lacking any basis of decency or compassion. Their lives are their own curse. I would like the killers to be caught. I wouldn't mind if the state killed them. But to me, people with that capacity for hate and cruelty are already dead. The Talmud says that those who are evil are dead when alive, and the righteous are alive, even when dead.

I have come to recognize that I best honor Koby by keeping his spirit alive. If I give in to anger and hate, then I become one of the haters, a parasite who lives on fear and hate. If I live only to seek revenge, then they have won; they have destroyed me. I will not let hatred tear me from the world and burn up my family. I will not let hatred reduce me to ashes.

Chapter twenty-one

Guilt

A mother who loses her child is bad. I am a guilty mother. I am a bad mother, one who has lost all she was supposed to protect and cherish.

There is the pain, and then there is the guilt. You can recover from the pain, but guilt can eat you everyday like acid. Rena tells me not to feel guilty. It wasn't my fault. "A mother is like a bus driver," she says. "Nothing happens without her, but she can't see behind her, what's going on."

But I did see behind. I drove along, looking at the rear view mirror, thinking I had my blind spot covered. I took rest stops and checked the children. I was a mother who always knew where my children were. I talked to them every day, trying to find ways to connect to their inner lives. I worked part-time so I could be home with them. I tried to make sure that I gave each one special time. And then I got hit. Now I am 'the bad mother.'

Today in downtown Jerusalem, I see an old man on a bicycle riding down an alley. There is a big truck ahead of him, blocking the alley. The bicyclist pushes on the truck with his hand, as if he could push the truck out of his way. And I understand how that truck is like guilt. And how I want to push it out of my way with just a pat. But it is there, waiting for me, waiting to be dealt with. And if I don't deal with it, it will block my way and keep me from moving.

The guilt of not being a good enough mother, every mother knows that one, but as my friend Shulamith says: There are plenty of lousy mothers and they don't lose their children, do they?

Guilt is so greedy. It would eat me up alive. It wants to eat up everything that it encounters, like Thing 1 and Thing 2 in *The Cat in the Hat*, appropriating everything for themselves. I always hated them, even as a kid. I hate chaos; I hate that which wants to suck us up alive and overwhelm us, swallowing us.

Why did I move here, to Tekoa? And why didn't I take Koby to town with me that day, and why didn't I talk to Koby before he went to sleep…Your last night when you wanted to talk…maybe you would have told me your plan and I could have persuaded you differently? Why didn't I know that you were cutting school, and why am I the one who has to suffer? What did I do wrong? I talked to Rabbi Twersky, a psychiatrist and addiction counselor, who told me: "You can survive the death, but guilt, guilt will kill you."

The guilt of bringing him here, where it was unsafe—that guilt may kill me, if I don't fight it. I thought I was in danger on the roads. I made sure he went on the bullet-proof bus. Many days I discouraged him from going to the mall in Jerusalem because I was afraid for him, afraid of a terrorist attack. I never imagined him in danger so close to home. Nobody had ever been hurt in the wadi or in Tekoa. Here in our settlement, I used to feel safe. But God is more creative than we are. What we worry about is rarely what we should worry about. God is too original for that.

We came with such hope. And now we have to live with the pain of our choice.

My husband and I hear a report on the radio about a man who kills himself during *Simchat Torah*, the same time of year his daughter was killed sixteen years ago. So many years ago and they link his suicide with his daughter's death. Because he thought he could have saved her. We bring them into the world, and it is our job to protect them.

Every parent who loses a child feels guilty, no matter how the child dies. Cancer, kidney failure, drowning, fire—there is something the parent feels he could have done to prevent the death. Seth tells me: If we had provided more of a framework for Koby he wouldn't be dead now. He means—if we had had dinner every night at six o'clock; if we had sat with him while he did his homework. If if if…the *if's* will kill you.

Rabbi Twersky said that as a lobster has to grow and shed its skin, so suffering allows us to grow. I am growing, despite myself. And Rena Ish-Ran's dream gives me comfort that I could not have stopped this death. Rena's dream helps me fight the guilt. Rena already knows the power of her dreams about her grandfather. Before she was married, she had a dream that her grandfather, who was already dead, came to her with a large straw basket of fruits and vegetables on his shoulders. He had brought them so they could make blessings on each one. When Rena told her mother the dream, her mother said, "Rena, it is a sign you will be married." Not long after, Rena met her husband.

A month before the boys die, Rena dreams that she is walking with her grandfather, a religious man, in the wadi. They walk on a path with rocks strewn all over. He leads her to a cave and says: "This is a bad house, a bad house." He keeps waving his hand around, gesturing wildly. "Leave this place, leave it." It is the cave where the boys were killed.

Rena says: "See, a month before, I knew. I saw it. But I didn't know what it meant."

Rena was moving houses in Tekoa at the time—from a temporary trailer that overlooked the wadi to a beautiful new house she had designed and had built. The day before Yosef was killed, she was buying paint the shade of blue he had requested for the walls of his room. She thought the dream meant something about moving out of the trailer and into the new house. But the dream was a premonition. Her grandfather was a holy man. His last name, in fact, Kadoshi, means holiness.

He was sending her a message, warning her, and perhaps preparing her for the impending blow. However, the message was undecipherable. I think the message was this: God has a plan and we humans can only know that plan once it has happened. Now we can read the dream clearly. But Rena couldn't have known before. Just as Moses could only see God from behind, we too can only see God's footprints once they are receding from us. We are not the supreme beings we believe ourselves to be. We are not all knowing, though we may try to be. To admit we are not in control, that's a hard one.

God, give me the strength and the wisdom to know: it wasn't my fault and for some reason, I had to come here.

We were drawn to Tekoa, and all of the circumstances conspired to send us here. Before we made *aliyah*, (literally, 'coming up', in the sense of ascending to Israel) after the Oslo accords, Seth said, "Maybe now, the boys won't have to go into the army."

We thought we would be safe. And, then when there were no rentals available in Efrat, and homes were being built in Tekoa, we moved and tried to buy a house. I thought that finally I could give my children a home in Israel. I wanted them to feel taken care of. I thought I could be a good mother by bringing them here, giving them a small, close-knit community of friends who would help them to become Israelis.

The guilt comes in waves. To fight it I have to realize that even if I was the best mother in the world, least selfish, most structured, most giving, most sensible, least narcissistic, most-attentive-to-my-kids mother, I could not have stopped this death. Even if I had kept Koby back in America. Maybe he would have died in a different way...maybe not in Tekoa, maybe not at all, but if God controls the world, then God called us here. I did not kill my son; terrorists did. Let me hold on to that so that I don't die from guilt each day.

Part two:
The Bird's Nest

Chapter twenty-two

Hope

My heart is like a safe that has been broken into. The door is swinging from its hinges, almost fallen off. There is no safe anymore. There is chaos and pain and treasures that have been taken—my son as well as the treasure of safety. The world is divided into people who have lost their loved ones, and those who haven't. People whose hearts have been broken and those whose haven't—people who have had their 'safe' broken into. Those in America now also hear the rumble of living each moment with insecurity. It is like living underneath a subway and trying to sleep. You know whenever you find a moment of silence, a train is racing its way closer, roaring into the station.

Still, with each day, I am trying to stitch myself back together. Rachel Naomi Remen says that each of us heals in our own way. Some people heal because they have work; others heal because they are released from work. Some people need music, others silence.

What I need are words and images and the time to be with my pain. It is as if I am writing my way out of the black hole of my despair and pain and anger. Through these words, I am healing. The words are a map; they are my path.

But I can't always listen to the words. Often, I want to hide in the cave with my son, beneath the ground. To heal I need my husband. Tonight he is on his way to Florida to give a speech. I don't know how I will be able to function without him. He carries the pain with me; it's not so heavy when he is here because we share it. We cope differently. He is already out in the world, speaking out, making a foundation in Koby's memory, channeling his pain into action.

I can accept his way and he can accept mine. But it is not easy for men and women to find a way to communicate about the pain they are carrying. Sometimes, neither can help the other. Robert Frost also lost his first-born son. His poem "Home Burial" is a powerful enactment of a lack of communication between husband and wife after the death of their child.

In the poem, the wife is upset with her husband, for his vigor in digging their child's grave; the way he comes into the house with the dirt from the grave still on his shoes and speaks afterwards about how rainy days can rot a birch fence. He pleads with her "let me into your grief" but the two stand alone, unable to share their pain. His wife addresses him:

> *You can't because you don't know how to speak.*
> *If you had any feelings, you that dug*
> *With your own hand—how could you?—his little grave;*
> *I saw you from that very window there,*
> *Making the gravel leap and leap in air,*
> *Leap up, like that, like that, and land so lightly*
> *And roll back down the mound beside the hole.*
> *I thought, Who is that man? I didn't know you.*

Thankfully, Seth and I, perhaps because I have so much support from my women friends, can support each other while we cope in our different ways. Usually, I want to stay home with the pain, writing, crying, being a housewife. Little rituals like folding the laundry which I used to disdain now connect me to the world, make me feel anchored in reality. Doing the dishes, sweeping the floor   mundane tasks help me feel that I can control pieces of my life.

Being out of my home can feel like a trial. When I am out in Jerusalem one month after Koby's death with Daniel, trying to buy him shoes, I start to cry and stare into the shop window. He looks at me impatiently and sadly. Suddenly, I have an idea of how to cry without hurting or scaring him. I give him my watch: "Time me, give me one minute to cry." He times me, I cry for twenty-two seconds. After that day when I cry, I give my children my watch. It becomes a sort of game. "Give me one minute," I tell them. I usually cry for barely twenty seconds. They see that pain is something that you can enter and not be destroyed by. It's okay to cry, to be sad. Accepting my pain means that I don't have to be afraid of it. Neither do my children or husband. The pain sometimes feels like panic and fear, like madness. But if you can find a way to let it live, you can bear it without being broken. Then you can begin to heal, sewing your life back together one stitch at a time.

Chapter twenty-three

Bird Stories

My nest is destroyed, and I have to build a new nest, a new way to protect my children. Birds and birds' nests have become symbols of healing for me. During the seven days of mourning, a friend told me I was like a bird with a broken wing, lying on the floor, almost too weak to move. Now I feel as if I am a bird that has flown from far away, migrated to a distant land. I could return, but I am staying in Israel, staying in this land of living with loss.

The birds help me. The birds teach me to build one twig at a time, even when I am weary. The birds show me I can continue to fly, and help my family fly, even when we feel stranded, even when I feel that like the dove Noah dispatched to see if the flood had subsided—there's nowhere to land.

One morning, I go to visit a friend, Shula, who is a widow. Her husband, a veteran of both the Israeli and American armies, died a year before Koby's murder. He'd suffered from cancer, but died suddenly, of heart failure. We talk and when I leave her house, I hear the birds and think: I need to go for a walk to listen to the birds. I need the healing sound of the birds, the sound that becomes texture.

As I walk I remember three stories about birds, three stories connected to Koby's life.

The first story is about a bird that was our pet and what the bird could teach us about peace.

The First Bird Story

My kids wanted a bird. I didn't like the idea of a bird with its spindly legs, its curved claws, and its sharp beak. I thought birds belonged outside, flying around, not caged inside a house.

Still my kids wanted one and my husband knew a little about birds since he had had one growing up. When we happened upon a plant store where they sold birds, we talked to the shop owner, who raised the birds himself, hand feeding them. Outside of the store was a cage with different sections for a variety of colorful birds: parrots, canaries, macaws and cockatiels. Daniel pointed to a yellow cockatiel with orange spots on his face. The proprietor said that one was promised to somebody; he was raising one like that now in his house; if we waited a few months, we could have one.

Each time we visited to check how our bird was doing, the man would give my kids a piece of chocolate or a balloon. He had a beautiful smile, curly black hair, dark skin. He always made us feel special. We enjoyed speaking with him about how our bird was coming along. Finally he called us with the news: we drove over to pick up our bird.

As soon as we got the cockatiel home, the kids tried to put him on my hand. "Get him away from me," I shouted. I had no interest in the bird, which the kids named Junior.

It took a long time. But slowly I began to feel affection for the bird. For one thing, he was beautiful, with dabs of yellow and orange on his head and belly. For another, he was sweet and gentle.

And then he began to be a friend. When I was home working during the day, he perched on the crossbars at the bottom of my computer chair where he was safe from being inadvertently knocked with my feet. When I read, he sat on my lap, raising his head so that I could stroke him under his beak.

He was free to fly through the house, perching on the bookshelves or on the breakfront. He became part of the family.

I had asked my husband to clip the bird's wings because Junior was able to fly around the house. And I thought he might fly right out an open door and into the trees outside. My prediction was right. The next day, then three-year-old son Gavi and his friend opened the cage and left the front door open. Junior flew away.

I told the kids to search the yard. I searched up and down the block. I looked for Junior's splotches of yellow and orange. I listened for his chirp. But I had never before noticed how full of birds my neighborhood is. Every tree and pole and bush was full of chirping birds.

I didn't know what to do. All those birds, all that chirping, all those trees. I felt utterly defeated. He could be anywhere.

The older kids were still at school. I had only two three-year-olds to help me. Then the Palestinian worker painting the house next door stepped out, his jeans smeared with white paint. This was in 1999, before the El Aksa intifada, during the days when we believed that peace was on the horizon.

"Are you looking for a bird?" he asked.

"Yes," I nodded.

"I saw him fly out, that way." He pointed. "I heard him," he said. "Come." I followed him in his paint-splattered clothes through backyards. He whistled for the bird as we looked in every tree, on every terrace, on each fence. "Let's look for the highest tree," he said. "He could be there."

In the intense midday heat, we walked through more backyards and some front yards, around people's houses, but we couldn't find the bird. I felt vulnerable in such isolated places with him, but I continued on.

"Maybe he'll fly home," he said. We walked back to my house.

I went into my house; he went into the house where he was

working. I started crying. I knew I would never see Junior again. The kids laughed at me. "We'll get another bird," they said.

I said, "I know I'm being silly but I don't want another bird. I want Junior." The loss filled me with sadness.

I went outside to hang out the laundry. I looked up. I saw a bird on an electric pole that looked a little like Junior. But it wasn't him.

I listened to the birds and realized how I had never really listened this closely before. As I hung out the laundry, the painter came outside again. He cocked his head.

"Listen," he said.

I didn't hear anything.

"It's him," he said. "I hear him."

I followed the man through the backyards again, the kids trailing behind. "Listen," he said. "You can hear him." But I couldn't hear anything. I couldn't distinguish one chirp from another. I couldn't tell.

He kept walking purposefully. Presently, he stopped in a backyard. "Look," he pointed. On the white trellis of a second floor terrace perched Junior, his yellow head cocked.

"It's him," I called. "It's him."

We quickly looked around for the owner of the house, but nobody was home. The painter boosted himself up, scaled the lattice outside of the house and stretched up to grasp Junior.

He cradled the bird with his hands and handed him to me.

I held Junior against me, close to my heart. He felt warm and soft.

"How did you do it? How could you find him? I was sure he was lost."

"You have to know how to listen," the painter replied.

"But I had given up," I said. "I had no hope."

He looked at me and shook his head.

We spoke then, about his wife and kids. About his village. I learned his name. Ibrahim. I learned he had left school at a very young age to help take care of his family. That he could hardly read and write.

The next day I saw Daniel, who has been afraid of Arabs, walk over to the house where Ibrahim was working. He called to Ibrahim and thanked him for saving his bird.

Maybe this is how peace will come, I thought. Slowly. People learning to listen. One bird at a time.

I was so innocent, so naïve. Even then, I had a feeling the bird story was only a story, a fairy tale. And now I know I was right. Because listening to each other isn't enough to create peace. There has to be a common language. A language where cruelty is not condoned, terrorism is not honored, and human life is respected.

The man who sold us the bird—I saw him after Koby was killed. At a meeting for relatives of dead children, killed by terrorism. He was with his elderly mother. Her daughter—and his sister—a forty-five-year-old teacher and a mother of six, had been shot dead by terrorists in a drive by shooting.

The Second Bird Story

A month after Koby is killed, Shulamith and I drive to the pool. On the way I tell her about my friends' dreams. In both of them Koby gives the person a message, saying he's okay. Mike, who has lived in Tekoa for over twenty years and is from England, comes to my house one night and relates the following dream: he is at a fair or at an amusement park. Suddenly he sees Koby. Koby is radiant; he is smiling and bouncing a ball. He says: "Hi Mike. Tell my mother it's really okay here. And it's very interesting."

Mike says he doesn't know what to make of the dream. He's never had a dream like this before. Maybe Koby went to him because they loved telling each other jokes. I smile. "It sounds like him," I say. "Koby got bored easily. That's why he liked studying *Gemorrah*. He needed things to be interesting."

The *Gemorrah* is part of the Oral Law, a commentary compiled between the years 200 and 500—which includes complex discussions of laws, stories and legends which have subsequently been commented on and argued over by rabbis throughout the centuries—a sort of chat room that spans centuries and continents. It was the one subject that Koby liked studying in school.

My friend Andrea, who has known Koby since the day he was born, has a dream. Her oldest son, Chaim, is one month older than Koby. They were friends as babies and when we returned seven years later from America, their reconnection was instant; their friendship became strong. Chaim hasn't been able to sleep well since Koby was killed.

In the dream, Koby is wearing a flowing white shirt with a few buttons at the neck and baggy white linen pants. "I was walking down a stone path and I came to a big iron gate," says Andrea. "Beyond the gate was an enormous white house that looked like a castle, with turrets, like in a storybook. The sun was glittering on the stones of the castle. I opened the gate. I was very nervous, on the verge of tears as I walked up to the door. Before I could knock, Koby opened the door. He looked beautiful and peaceful, taller. He was barefoot. His skin was clear, almost translucent and his hair was a lighter color, like when he was a baby. He gave me a smile, which was like the smile a parent gives a child who is suffering for no reason. I said, 'Koby, are you okay?' He communicated telepathically. He didn't say it with his mouth—but I heard it. 'Tell Chaim I'm okay.'"

"It's weird," I say to Shulamith in the car. "Both of them had the same message."

"Those are classic dreams," Shulamith says to me in the car. Shulamith is a therapist, originally from Mexico City, who has worked extensively with dreams. "Because the person who has passed on cannot contact loved ones who are in so much pain, he communicates with others."

The way I understand it is that the pain creates static that's so loud that one can't receive the messages directly.

I say: "But I want him to contact me. I want him to come to me."

Suddenly a bird smashes against the windshield of the moving car—bang—and then flies off into the sky, perfectly unhurt.

"There he is," says Shulamith. "He came to you. You've just got to believe it."

Oh God, I want to believe it. But I want Koby, not a bird bumping my moving car.

The Third Bird Story

The first time we go as a family to visit the grave alone, I am prepared for a terrible unleashing of pain, a volcano of fear and dread and horror. We get out of the car and walk toward the grave. Instead of walking on the paved path from the parking lot, the kids scamper down a hill filled with pine trees. Gavi meets us at the grave, holding a feather with iridescent blue stripes, small, perfect, an intricate crosshatching. He says, "This is for Koby, to make his soul happy."

The children spike the feather into the ground at Koby's grave, as if they are planting it there, and then put a rock over the feather so that it doesn't blow away. They say: "We'll see if it's here next time." I look around, at the pines, and the light blue sky filled with soft tender clouds, and I think: what a beautiful place is this world. I take out my prayer book and turn to this page: *The heavens declare the glory of God... and the expanse of the sky tells of God's handiwork. Day unto day utters speech, and night unto night declares knowledge.* (Psalm 19, verses 2–3)

Suddenly I realize that nature is God's speech. But you have to know how to listen.

Chapter twenty-four
Thanksgiving Blessings

E ven though I am an Israeli, I am also an American, and Thanksgiving is a holiday we like to celebrate. On Thanksgiving we are supposed to give thanks. A website asks me to write an article on Thanksgiving. But what does it mean—to give thanks? How can I give thanks?

If being thankful means that I need to accept what has happened to me, then I can't be grateful. But maybe being grateful means being grateful for what I have and not dwelling on what I don't have, being humble enough to accept what I am given.

Being grateful is so difficult. When my kids were babies, I was grateful to have survived another day. It was so much work taking care of little kids. They wore me out so much that sometimes I would put them in the car just to drive around and get them to sleep.

But how can I be grateful now? I am forced to reconsider the whole notion of blessing. If the Torah tells us we are blessed, what does it mean for me? When Isaac blessed his children, "his eyes were dim so that he could not see." We also are supposed to close our eyes when we bless our children every Friday night after blessing the wine at the Sabbath table. One reason is so that we see our children as whole and overlook their faults, not seeing anything wrong with them. Now I understand. Blessing doesn't mean that we get what we want. It can mean letting go of what we think we want so that we can recognize the gifts we are given. Discovering blessing starts with accepting imperfection, in God's world, and in others and ourselves.

Occasionally, I had a hard time accepting Koby. Because he was my oldest, I thought he should be more helpful, better behaved, play the role of the perfect big brother. My battle with imperfection usually rested on his shoulders. I found it much easier to accept the minor faults of my other kids, much more difficult to accept him totally because he was more of a challenge in many ways. For example, Koby could choose to be magnificently lazy, like a prince. He never felt rushed or hurried. The moment was so precious to him he didn't ever risk spoiling it with chores or studying.

He wasn't always lazy, though. Once, I came home and found that he had cleaned out a year's worth of caked-on ice from the freezer. He would take care of his younger brother whenever I asked him. He would run to go pick up a pizza. Once, when we were out for a walk, he carried Gavi home for me, on his shoulders, rollerblading for over a mile. The thing was, he chose when he wanted to move. Not always easy for a mother to handle.

Getting ready for the Jewish holidays could be especially frustrating. To get him to help was very difficult. I would get angry with him, especially when I saw all the neighbors' children helping like little worker ants. And then I would get even more upset, because I felt his laziness labeled me an inadequate mother. And in fact, now that I think about it, the reason he upset me so much is because I too am lazy in just the same ways he is lazy.

But now, now as we get ready for Sabbath and holidays and I don't have Koby to yell at to help, I realize: just when the pain of missing him is a constant knife to my heart, his laziness is a gift to me. Because as we go through the holidays, I can't think: If only Koby were here to help us. Because I know that he would be lazing in his bed eating chips and salsa and I would be yelling at him.

I can't turn him into a saint. I remember him too clearly.

But now I see his laziness in a different light. I recognize something I wasn't ready to see before: there was also a positive part of his unwillingness to get up and work with me.

I could have learned something from him: how to be in the moment; how not to care what other people think; how to enjoy life; how to relax, how to forgive. In short, I could have accepted his nature more. I could have even been grateful that I had a kid whose biggest problems with me I perceived as a messy room and an inability to work when I wanted him to. Now the fact that he didn't help helps me. Because it forces me to remember him as a real person.

Miraculously, I begin to understand how we should bless the bad as we bless the good. I see glimmers that I will learn to accept the life I have been given, to put my hands on my life and close my eyes and see it as the wholeness with which I have been blessed.

Chapter twenty-five

First Born

Losing the first born means losing a double blessing. The power of the first child is recognized by Jewish law, which stipulates that the oldest, the *bachur*, receives double the inheritance. Some commentators claim this inheritance is in compensation for the firstborn's status as guinea pig for inexperienced parents. But more likely, the eldest receives the double inheritance because he receives twice the attention of the other children. His parents bask in him, but at the same time try to subdue him. As a result, he learns about power, how to wield it and how to fight it. Many of the astronauts are first born, so are the presidents—the first child is born to be in the spotlight.

Koby was definitely in the center of my stage. As a new mother, I witnessed each milestone of Koby's growth as a revelation. When he walked, I felt like Neil Armstrong had just stepped on to the moon. When Koby talked, it was as if speech had just been invented.

He trained me in child rearing. I had no idea of how to take care of a baby. Could I let him nurse all day? What should I do when he wanted to walk the stroller instead of ride in it? Why was he biting me? How I could answer without anger, lead without force, allow his individuality to blossom? Because Koby was sheer power, always bumping into us, making us pay attention. Look at our family photographs; there you will see Koby at the center of things, making faces, putting his long arms around the other kids, hamming it up. The other children lean toward him, attracted to his power.

He was always ahead of himself and sometimes of me as well. When he was a baby in a car seat, no more than the age of two, he pointed the way to our "Mommy and me" playgroup, and pestered me until I turned the way he pointed. He was right about the direction.

When Koby was eleven and we were in the car, he told me that I needed to shift from third gear to fourth. I said: "When did you learn to drive?" But I shifted and the car drove more smoothly.

He knew things. He knew what he wanted to do with the money his grandmother gave him for his *bar mitzvah*—invest it all in Microsoft. He understood how the stock market worked, even though we had no money invested in it. He even had comments about my parenting skills. He read my parenting books—especially Faber and Mazlish's *How to Talk so Kids will Listen, and How to Listen so Kids will Talk*. He would tell me what I was doing wrong with him and the other kids. For example, he'd jokingly say "Don't yell at them...describe the situation...say I see the children and one truck. What do we do now?" (as suggested in the book). I would laugh at my co-disciplinarian.

We shared so much. He was like an ally. He read my articles and commented on them, telling me what to cut, what to keep, and how to change the words. He liked reading my women's magazines and making fun of the *100 Ways to Make Your Husband Love You* type articles. He read the Hardy Boys and Harry Potter over and over until he had them memorized. When he was two, he could already recite his books by heart. Also, when he was two, he walked out of the house, and went to the park by himself.

He was a challenge. Once, when he was seven, we had moved and he was so upset, he ran away and got lost, and we had to call the police. He walked in the door a few minutes later, driven home by people who had found him. One night in anger, he kicked out the window of a house we lived in.

Sometimes I feel that he is still making us pay attention to him, too much attention. Sometimes the other kids are still jealous of him.

He was never easy. But he was so loving and strong. Whenever I was with Koby, I felt safe. He seemed invulnerable to me. He hardly wore a coat; he was never cold. When the rest of the family got hepatitis soon after making aliyah, he was the only one who didn't.

Until Koby was two, we lived in Israel. We moved back to America because I wasn't prepared to be Israeli at that point—I'd come on vacation and ended up living in the country for seven years. I was afraid of the danger of bringing up my children in Israel, and I wasn't ready to accept and live in the harsher culture of Israel where everything—work, school, shopping, driving—was more of a struggle. I missed simple things like carpeting and the radio in English. I wanted to be in a society I understood. Plus, I wanted to be closer to my family. So Seth got a job as a Hillel director (serving the spiritual, emotional and educational needs of Jewish students on campus), first at Penn State and then later at the University of Maryland. I taught writing at both universities. We had satisfying jobs, friends, a decent house, but somehow something was missing and Koby felt it too. He felt our need for Israel, for a deeper spiritual life more tied to Jewish culture and Torah.

When Koby was in nursery school, the teacher made a book with the children's answers to questions—What do you want to learn? Where do you want to visit? While most of the children wanted to learn to play hockey or a game on the computer, Koby wanted to learn Hebrew. While the other kids wanted to visit Disneyland or Florida, Koby wanted to visit Jerusalem. Israel was in his soul.

But after seven years in the states, coming back to Israel was tough. Koby started fourth grade, and went from being in a class of fifteen well-behaved boys and girls to a class of forty raucous Israeli boys, but he never complained. He couldn't speak or understand what was going on. The kids didn't make friends, didn't learn the language, and we didn't find jobs. We were living in Efrat, a town some twenty minutes drive from Jerusalem that had been founded in the early 1980s, by Rabbi Shlomo Riskin, an American rabbi. We thought the transition would be easier because there were lots of Americans. But even the American kids didn't speak English in school. Koby was left to manage on his own there.

It was hard on everybody, but especially on Koby, since he was the oldest. But he knew Israel was his place and that it was an honor to live here. The fact that he was a good athlete helped. Even if he couldn't speak, he could play soccer, so the boys accepted him. Still, I remember the first summer when we lived in Efrat, walking by the library and seeing Koby in there alone, reading. He looked so sweet. But I felt guilty as well. He'd had so many friends in Silver Spring, Maryland where we'd moved from, and had been so popular, and I'd dragged him here and now he was alone. Even so, I thought, maybe being a popular, outgoing, smart kid thrown into difficult circumstances, basically becoming one of the least popular kids, would make him more sensitive, more compassionate.

During those years, Koby was home a lot, reading. It took him a long time to find friends. So I got to spend a lot of time with him, to enjoy him. Sometimes it was magic together. A month or so before he was killed, we stood in the kitchen and spontaneously told a story together, me giving a sentence, and then him, weaving a story from the air. And I realized: he added brilliance and originality and coherence to my narrative.

The night before he was killed, I asked him to baby-sit so I could go to a women's Torah class, but he was too busy. Finally, he had a group of friends, he was starting to fit in. I was relieved. I was supposed to go into town to a party for the editor of Hadassah magazine who was in from New York, but somehow I couldn't go, the hours crept past and I didn't feel that I could leave my family. The roads were dangerous; I wanted to be home.

Something kept me home so that I could have my last hug and kiss from Koby. He came upstairs and gave me a huge hug and kiss and said "You're so beautiful mom," teasing my vanity, knowing how much I enjoyed being told that. I'd already said goodnight to him downstairs though, so I didn't understand why he came up specially to say good night again.

Now I think that he felt guilty about his plans for the next day, perhaps wanting to give me a little more love because he knew he was planning on doing something naughty. Perhaps he wanted me to stop him, to talk him out of it.

I get so angry with him. Why did he have to be so fearless, so stupid? I want to shake him: go back to school. I want that day back so I can make sure that he boards the bus, sits in class, eats his salami sandwiches, comes home, walks in the door, throws his jacket and books on the floor and screams: I'm hungry! But kids went down to the wadi all the time. In fact, that day there were people there rappelling, other people walking.

It's strange, but in the Torah no first son keeps his privileged position. Yishmael is displaced by Isaac, Esau by Jacob, Menashe by Ephraim. That position is so delicate, that power so vulnerable. In the Torah, the person who fulfills the destiny of the firstborn is not the one for whom it was originally designated.

And your power is not lost. Because there is power in your death. And the power has to do with another characteristic of the firstborn. In the Bible, the firstborn is designated to serve in the temple, to represent the family in making sacrifices, to represent the family in holiness.

I feel called on to continue pursuing your destiny with you. According to the *Zohar*, each soul has a mission in this world. Normally, a soul can only acquire a new mission when a person dies and the soul is later born into a different body. But if a person undergoes a near death experience, a new soul may be brought down into that person's body. It is literally as if the person has been reborn. In suffering my son's murder, I've also been reborn. I am not the same person, I've acquired a new mission in life. Koby is leading us to a new sense of holiness, still bumping against us, forcing us to define ourselves, creating a deeper belief in God and in our mission on this earth.

A rabbi I spoke with said that everyone lives with the awareness of evil. But once you are forced into an intimate acquaintance with evil, then your mission in the world changes. You are called upon to fight evil. Koby, your death has given us a new mission—to take your strength and bring it out into the world, your love of Israel, your love of being Jewish, your belief in God. I remember asking you—do you really believe in God, and you answered: How could I not? It was part of you. The belief that everything is for a purpose. I have a new purpose, and I will not waver from it—to take all of the unbearable cruelty of your death, to take the evil, and transform it into love and kindness, the love you had for the world. In your honor, I will take the double blessing you were born with—and send it out to the world.

Chapter twenty-six
Chanukah

Koby was murdered at the age of thirteen, a prime number. Prime numbers are a special category. Nothing else can enter them. My son's death is like a prime number, divisible only by itself.

Will Koby always be thirteen? Does he age in heaven? To attach a number to him is meaningless. He has left the world of numbers. I have a friend whose twenty-two-year-old brother was in a coma for thirteen years. It was exceedingly painful for her to see her brother age, his hairline recede. His body was a shell for his soul. He was still in the world of numbers, but there was no category that fit him.

When I am asked how many children I have, how should I answer? Do I count Koby? How can I not? How can a number describe my desire for him?

There is a picture in my daughter's room that shows Koby and me together at a *Bar Mitzvah*, two months before he was killed. What I see in my eyes is how proud I was to be his mother, how proud that a brilliant, beautiful child like Koby was in my life. I had such a feeling of ownership with him. I felt like he was mine, almost like I had created him. Though now, I see, I never owned him. Because if I had, I would never have allowed him to be taken from me and from this world.

I used to think that life was about acquiring and creating and keeping things whole. But now, when my arm still reaches for four chocolate pudding treats on the shelf of the supermarket even though one of my four children is dead, I see that life is about learning how to see in the darkness.

Chanukah is also about learning a new way of seeing. The Maccabee's war against the Hellenists was a fight not just for territory but also for a worldview. The Greeks believed in the grace of beauty, the redemptive powers of humanity; the Maccabees in the justice and goodness of God. For the Hellenists, the body was perfection; for the Maccabees, the body was an instrument to be used for serving God.

The Maccabees insisted on giving tribute to God and his laws, and his temple. When the Maccabees were victorious and reclaimed the temple, there was just a little oil left to light the menorah, enough for one day. They kindled the flame and the oil lasted for eight days. Many people believe that this is the miracle of Chanukah.

But maybe it wasn't a miracle at all. Perhaps one vial of oil can always be enough for eight nights if we look at our lives as a place for God to dwell. Because God is infinite, when we approach divinity, we leave the world where numbers circumscribe reality. Once we make a sanctuary for God, then the infinite possibilities of God dwell within us as well. Numbers become guides, instead of rulers.

Chanukah teaches us that what we see in this world is a glimmer of the truth. Our measurements in this world are imprecise, our ways of knowing limited. The world of truth is not one where the numbers we ascribe to reality are sufficient. One vial of oil becomes eight. Thus it is fitting that Chanukah begins during the month of Kislev, the month of dreams and sleep. Nearing the winter solstice, we prefer more and more to stay in bed. Many of the Torah portions of this month speak of sleep and dreams—Jacob has his dream of a ladder and God speaking to him; Pharaoh has dreams that need to be interpreted.

Chanukah itself has the logic of a dream. In sleep we have access to a different world—a world where what is impossible during the day becomes possible. In sleep, the few can become many. The light at night is a deeper light with a greater capacity for revelation. This is the light of Chanukah. This is the light of holiness.

It's not easy to see in the dark, but you don't need that much oil to fill the darkness. A small measure can easily expand to light the largest cavern. The kaballah tells us that we are like flames, the spark of our souls reaching toward the candle of God.

To see God in my life, I have to see in the darkness—to see beyond what appears to be, to stop counting with ordinary integers of ownership—to see what is blurred, undefined, beyond my ordinary senses. Chanukah tells me that what matters is not how old Koby is now—I can't count him anymore with my daytime logic. What matters is that I consecrate the light of his soul so that it shines within me.

Chapter twenty-seven

Faith

Six months after your death, my body has phantom legs that walk to your bed to wake you for synagogue. My body lags in recognizing your absence. It is still moving toward you, like a flower to the light. The phantom legs walk to the door to welcome you home from school, bring you chips and salsa when you return.

As I walk up to the synagogue, I see your friends, who are starting to fill out, getting huskier now as they get taller. They are beginning to look more like men than boys. Seth says he can see them grow each week, can tell the minute differences in them from week to week, how their shoulders are filling out, how they are taller, wider, their features becoming more chiseled. And the pain of the loss, forever expanding, spreads inside of me like a flame in a forest of trees during years of drought.

I walk into synagogue and sit with friends. I am cushioned from the pain because men and women sit separately—I never sat next to Koby in synagogue. Seth did. For Seth, synagogue is a hammer against his forehead. Seeing the boys makes him yearn for his son.

I look over the divider between the men's section and the

women's section at shul and remember watching Koby across the synagogue praying. He stands next to the open window with a view of the cone shaped mountain of Herodian, King Herod's palace. Koby prays with such fervor I wonder to myself: From where did this believer come? He is wearing a blue shirt though it's traditional here to wear a white shirt in synagogue. I remember the first time we prayed in Efrat, right after coming to live in Israel. The first *Shabbat* Seth and the kids went to synagogue, the four hundred men and boys there were all wearing white shirts. Except for Koby. When they came out of shul, Seth said to him: "You know, for next week, you should think about changing your shirt."

Koby looked at him and asked: "Why?"

He didn't notice what everybody else was doing. He didn't need to. He didn't need approval. He wasn't different on purpose to bump up against things. He was just naturally himself, genuinely unconcerned about what other people were doing. He decided what was right for him. He liked blue, so he wore it.

For that reason, he wasn't embarrassed to be with me, even in public, even though he was a teenager. He didn't care if it wasn't "cool" to be with your mother. I didn't embarrass him as I do my other now-teen children.

When I was a child, I never went to synagogue. Occasionally, I went because my friends, who were forced to attend, were there on Saturday morning. But I never went into the prayer sanctuary. I went to the ladies room. My friends would sit in the bathroom and try to levitate people. Or we would smoke cigarettes and try out the potions and lotions left over from the gift basket in the bathroom after somebody's wedding. Prayer never occurred to me.

Now, I go to the prayer book and there is my story. I read the Psalms, which I once disdained, and there is my story. These books speak to me with the force of tragedy and redemption. "Favor me God because I am feeble; heal me God because my bones shudder with terror. My soul is utterly terrified, and You, God, how long? …Save me as befits your kindness. For there is no mention of you in death, in the grave who will praise you? I am wearied with my sigh, every night

I drench my bed with my tears, I soak my couch. Depart from me all evildoers for God has heard the sound of my weeping." (Psalm 6)

My story is an old story, one the Jews have suffered before, one that painfully keeps repeating. But I feel that God hears me weeping. God hurts when I cry. I pray but I keep confusing God and Koby. I pray to God to protect my son, to save him, but what can that mean now? I pray to God to take care of him now the way I cared for him. The truth is: I don't know how to speak to God about Koby. What can I ask Him for? That He be near him, that He protect him? I don't know what that means up in heaven exactly. So I pray to Koby to help us, to help me with the pain, to help me and the children and my husband continue.

I struggle to hold on to my belief in the justice of God's world. I struggle to believe that God is good. I cannot believe otherwise. What occurs to us is not an accident. How could it be—when the whole world is so clearly orchestrated—that we, too, are not also part of the symphony? And though only our hearts can hear the music, I think the birds hear it in the morning, and that's why they begin to sing.

In my soul, I yearn now for redemption, for that which is holy, to bring the highest part of myself to act in the world. That is why I need the words in the prayer book. I pray to God who, in the words of the morning blessings 'clothes the naked'—to put a blanket on my raw pain. I pray to God who 'releases the bound,' to release me from the staggering pain, the reeling, sinking into despair. I pray to God who 'gives strength to the weary.' I am tired, stone-tired with anguish. And I pray that God will keep me alive, keep me strong, "firm my footsteps, gird me with strength."

Suddenly, as I pray, I remember watching Koby on the day of his *Bar Mitzvah*. That day he also wore blue. His blue shirt stood out like the blue strand on the *tzizit*, the ritual garment that all religious males over the age of three wear. This garment, worn under clothing, reminds us to remember God's commandments. On each corner, some wear a thread of blue, blue to remind us of the sky and the sea, of infinity. In the book *A Thread of Blue*, written after her teenage son's death, Judy Belsky compares her son's death to this thread. Death is like a blue thread that highlights the white of the prayer shawl, the rest of our life. "The gift of the thread of blue is all the pain and all the privilege we can find in living."

When your eye is drawn to the blue of the prayer shawl, to the contrast between what remains and what is gone, you look at the world differently. In my journal, I wrote this after Koby died: "All I want is broken and no matter how hard I try I can't fix it. I will be hanging from a noose, swinging there alive the rest of my life because you are dead."

Each time I choose life, it is as if I rise up from the dead to be given new life. The white of ordinary life offers itself as an anchor and a comfort, a bed with sheets fresh from the wash and the breeze blowing the curtains; moments enhanced by my perception of pain into moments of solace. The white of regular life shines in relief to the pain we carry. We learn to cherish our children, our husbands. Getting my child ready for school in the morning, making him a cup of tea can feel like a privilege. That is the beauty of the blue thread.

Sherri, with friend and counselor Shira (left)

Chapter twenty-eight

The Language of God

God is speaking to me. I know that. But sometimes his voice is silent. Other times he mumbles. I have to keep learning, so that I can recognize his language. I have to keep my heart open, so that I can receive God's divinity.

When the angels came to Abraham, his tent was open on all four sides, to welcome visitors. Even though he'd had his circumcision three days earlier and was in pain, he welcomed the guests eagerly into his tent, and quickly fed them and bathed their feet. In the Bible, it says: And God appeared to him (Abraham) beneath the trees of Mamre as he was sitting before the door of his tent in the heat of the day. He lifted up his eyes and saw, and lo, three men were standing there, turned toward him..." (Genesis 18:1–2).

It is not clear if God appears first, and then the three men, or if, in an alternative reading, the three men themselves are God, that is agents, or angels of God. For the word angel in Hebrew, *malach*, means a messenger, somebody sent as an emissary of God with a message in this world.

It seems that wherever I look now, I see these messengers. My angels were here, assembled, waiting for me, though I didn't know it at the time.

First and foremost, there is my friend Shira. Though trained as a pastoral counselor, in Israel she is a massage therapist and my kids' English teacher. Ever since Koby was murdered, she has become my live-in therapist. For the first two months, she came to my house every single day to speak with me—to find out how my day had been. Grief can feel like panic and fear, anxiety that borders on madness. Many days I felt I would plunge into a whirlpool of pain and that I would drown there. But knowing she was coming to speak to me, allowed me the luxury of plunging into the pain, knowing someone was there to rescue me.

A few months after Koby was killed, I went to a house of mourning of someone I didn't know—Miriam. Her sixteen-year-old daughter, Shoshi, was killed when terrorists shot at the bus taking her home from high school in Jerusalem. I sat next to Miriam. She hadn't eaten or slept in three days, she told me. A woman a bit older than me with kind eyes and a soothing voice spoke to Miriam and told her that a piece of her own heart was broken too. Then she said: "Please call me if you want to talk." I told that woman: "You call Miriam. She needs you." Shira taught me that. Shira taught me that you reach out to someone in pain. You go to her and you provide a place for her to express her pain. You don't pat her and you don't tell her everything is going to be okay. You say it hurts, it's a horrible pain, it's a pain that people can't see but it's there and it doesn't hurt any less. It will take as long as it takes.

Two months after Koby is murdered, Shira tells me "You are a two-month old baby. You have to learn to crawl and to walk again. You need to be carried." She carries me. She lets me grieve. She recognizes my authentic being—grieving mother—and pays tribute to it by allowing me to express it fully without fear or embarrassment. It is what we all need, grieving or not—someone who will listen and recognize who we are, not who they would like us to be; someone who will love us in our pain, in our sorrow, in our nakedness.

I have another angel: Valerie, the mother of seven, who calls me five times every day; who was here night and day during the *shiva*; who came to my house to make me scrambled eggs each morning, who invited me to dinner every Sabbath. Every day for the first year she called me. She gave me unconditional love like a mother. She knew what to say, and what not to say. She wasn't afraid of my pain and she didn't minimize it or discount it. She never stopped helping. She still hasn't.

Sometimes people say to me—I don't know what to say. But a neighbor who didn't know what to say came to my house and washed my clothes, cleaned my house, hung my laundry. One night I walked downstairs, and another neighbor, a Harvard graduate, was washing my floors, cleaning my bathroom. You may not have words, but everybody has something to offer those in grief, something essential from their own being. There is something inside of everybody to give—if they are not afraid of the pain on the other side.

The people who helped me aren't real angels. I know that. But it is said that God sends angels to help you when you are about to stumble. Without my angels, I fear that I would still be in bed, afraid of the light, afraid of contact, afraid of anyone seeing the tear inside of me.

Angels can come to us anywhere, but we have to be willing to recognize the divine message that each person can give us. Many of us are angels but we balk at our jobs. Because to be an angel, you also have to believe you have something to give. Sometimes I feel that each moment is an opportunity to encounter an angel. Because nothing happens twice, everything in our world is in the process of unfolding; each moment is a unique revelation. When you look at the world like that, it keeps giving to you.

Because of my angels, I can bear my pain. I can walk with it. I see that even in suffering, there is love. The pain can be so overwhelming that it is too hard to carry alone. But my angels help me carry it. Of course, I will always long for my son. But there is beauty in my pain, beauty in the hands that are extended to me. A hole can be tattered and frayed or it can be woven into fabric, like lace. In his collection *Great Tranquility,* in the poem, "Lying in Wait for Happiness," Yehuda Amichai says:

> "...my soul is rent and torn like yours
> but it is beautiful because of that
> like fine lace."

Chapter twenty-nine

Signs and Dreams

On *Simchat Torah*, the holiday when we complete the yearly cycle of reading the Torah and begin the cycle anew, I can hardly move. I remember this festival from previous years, Koby holding Gavi on his shoulders, dancing in the synagogue, going round and round; holding Gavi's best friend, Zevi, holding other children, his face flushed and happy. I can't even bear the name of the day, a name with happiness in it. How can I survive this day? A day with happiness makes me feel like sticking daggers into trees.

The doorbell rings and it's Tanya, an artist from South Africa who has three small children. She wants to know how I am. I know that her mother died young of breast cancer. I ask Tanya if she's had any signs from her mother. "Only one," she says. "It was the Sabbath after she died. I lit candles and I prayed, God please give me a sign. All of a sudden the doorbell rang. I ran to the door, but no one was there. We lived in a house with a long walkway to the entrance. If anyone was there, I would have seen them. No one was there."

I'll accept Elijah, the Messiah, angels, crickets, shooting stars. But ringing doorbells sound supernatural to me. It seems bizarre.

Then a week later, I walk into my friend Valerie's house. Suddenly the doorbell rings. The door is still open from my entrance. No one is there. Valerie says, "That's strange. We don't even have a doorbell."

What she means is that the button of the bell is missing. A jumble of wires juts from the open button of the bell. "We would have heard if someone had come," Valerie says. I look up the steps. Nobody is there.

"It's Koby," Valerie says.

Well, I think, skeptically, a doorbell and a cricket have something in common. They both wake you up. It could be they are trying to wake me up to strengthen my belief in the life of the soul. Koby wants me to believe in our connection. "I'm here Ma," he seems to be saying, "I'm still here."

Then he comes to me in a dream to tell me so.

In my dream, I have a brand new baby. The baby is only a few days old, but he is already walking. "What an advanced baby," I think to myself. I count my children. I have five children now and they are all here. I feel wonderful, like everything has been put back into place. Koby says: "Mommy, I have a test in school. I need you to drive me." So I leave the other kids and drive him to the school. We walk into the school office. The secretary directs him to the classroom where he is to take the test. As he walks toward the test, he turns to me. He says: "Mommy, I need you to stay with me while I take the test."

I have a lot to do at home, I think. But still, if I need to stay, I'll stay.

He smiles at me and leaves the room to take the test.

I sit in the office and wait for him. When I wake up, I feel relieved. I am with him but he is also with me. I can't see him; he's in the other room taking the test. But I know he will pass the test. I am also taking a test. My test is the faith to continue and believe that Koby is with me even though I can't see him. I will pass my test, because we are taking our tests together.

Chapter thirty

The Family

I t's hard for the one who dies, but it's harder for those left behind,"
Koby said after two high school boys were killed by terrorists only
two months before his own death.

Now it is like our family was tossed high into the sky and
is tumbling down, trying to hold hands but being forced apart at
times as we reposition ourselves into a different arrangement. We
are falling—sometimes gently, sometimes violently, and we have
parachutes—routine, friends, our faith, our work—that allow us to
cushion our landing. But at times, too often, our parachutes don't
release and we are in free fall, wondering how we will possibly land
without fracturing all of the bones of our body. And if we land, we
do not know how our feet will hold us and allow us to walk on the
ground with all we have lost.

My friend Hadassah, who has ten kids, once told me that
she loves all of her kids, not more or less, but differently. I can love
nobody the way I love Koby. My husband and my children can love
no one the way they loved Koby. And they will never be loved in the
same way—by Koby.

Our standing in the world is shaken. Evil is in front of our faces; death is in our beds. The night of the funeral, I go to Eliana, ten years old, to comfort her. We are in her room, on her bed. Her hair is dark and tussled; her eyes look at me with infinite kindness. She rubs my back, asks me if she can bring me tea. I tell her: "I'm the mother and I'm here to take care of you."

She says: "No, I'm your mother."

I say, "No, I am still your mother and this is very hard now, but we will get through it, we will go on, and I will still be your mother."

"No," she says, "I'll be your mother."

"No, I am the mother, and I know it's hard, but you are my child, and I will take care of you," I say firmly.

"Okay," she says, "I'll be your grandmother."

A few months later, a filmmaker asks Eliana about her memories of Koby. He wants to film her. She refuses. Once, a news crew filmed her without her permission. She has already experienced the intrusion of the media. She has a sense already of how the media can steal you, your purity, your soul. Seth and I are on camera, talking about Koby, about how wonderful he was, how smart, how funny. When I go inside, she tells me: "He wasn't an angel, you know." She is the voice of truth, the voice that refuses to make him bigger than he was in life. She tells the filmmaker she has no special memories of Koby. He was her brother; they ate together, fought together. He was no hero for her. She misses the everyday Koby, the one she sat at dinner with, the one who teased her friends.

To six-year-old Gavi, he was a hero. Koby took care of Gavi a lot, especially the one year I worked full time as a writer for a website. They were eight years apart and had no sibling rivalry. Gavi speaks in Koby's phrases—"That's really sick!" he'll say, mimicking Koby. Or he'll tell a joke that Koby told him. In losing Koby, Gavi and I have lost a pure love.

A month and a half after the murder, I take Gavi with me on a walk with my friend, Shira. Our dog is with us, unchained. Gavi says, "Put him on the leash." I tell him it's okay, I always walk her without a leash.

We can see the wadi from the road where we are walking. Gavi starts crying. "You want her to die?"

I say, "No. I don't want her to die."

He says, "She's going to get into a fight and die. Don't you worry about her?"

I say, "I do worry and nothing will happen to her. Are you afraid?"

And then he tells me how he is afraid of the Arabs in the wadi—they could come up and kill us too. Shira says that we have security patrolling in the wadi now. He says, "Well a boy could go down there and hide behind a rock."

I tell Gavi, "I worried about Koby and I worry about you and I will try my best not to let anything happen to you and Koby didn't die because of me or because of you, Gavi. He died because the Arabs beat him."

I want to be able to say that I won't let anything happen to him. But already at the age of six, he knows that I cannot protect him from all evil.

Daniel, twelve, is invited to summer camp in America. On arrival, he refuses to unpack. The head counselor calls me and asks what to do. I say—he doesn't have to unpack. The next day Daniel calls. He is watching boys Koby's age play basketball and he is crying thinking of how much Koby loved basketball, how much Koby would love being at the camp. At home, he sleeps in our room on the floor. He needs to feel safe. He needs our presence.

At the *shiva*, a well-known politician came to our home. I introduced all of my children to him. He looked at Daniel and asked him how old he was: "So now, you're the *bechur*," he told him, "you're the oldest."

"No," Daniel shook his head. "I'm not. Koby will always be the *bechur*."

Koby will always be our eldest son.

I feel sorry for the pain my children already know. A newspaper reporter from Scotland tells me she feels sorry for my children. I tell her there's a lot to feel sorry for. But maybe this tragedy will make them into even greater people with bigger hearts and wide-open eyes. Maybe if I show them we can live with the tragedy, so we make more of our lives, well then, maybe his death won't just hurt them, but will help them too. They already know the worst life has to offer. They have seen the evil in the world; they know how death lurks behind everything. To have such knowledge at such a young age could mean they can go forth as agents of blessing in this world.

Chapter thirty-one

The Reporters

On September 13, 2001, I have my first TV interview. I would not speak to television for six months after Koby's death. My grief was private, my sorrow my own. I didn't want to share it and I didn't want others to bask in it. But now I am ready to speak. I can shield my feelings; I can protect my pain because I want to share with others what I have learned.

The occasion is the presentation of a *Rosh HaShana* card for the Jewish New Year, from the kids of America to the kids of Israel. It is the largest *Rosh HaShana* card ever made—thousands of kids' drawings and messages mounted on boards in Safra Square, at Jerusalem's town hall.

The project is the brainchild of Toby Herzog, a twenty-three-year-old woman from Baltimore. She wants American kids to connect to Israel and she has spearheaded this effort of good will. But the ceremony, which has been long planned, comes just two days after the World Trade Center attacks. So the *Rosh HaShana* card now has new meaning. In fact, during the ceremony, Ehud Olmert, the mayor of Jerusalem, addresses the people of New York and tells them that we are with them in their pain, that we understand what they are going through. "Today we are all New Yorkers," he says. A street in Jerusalem will be renamed New York Street for the next month.

My son, Daniel, also delivers a speech. In his speech, he accepts the card in memory of Koby and in memory of all who were killed this past year. He thanks the kids of America for paying attention to us. He says that he knows that when you are hurt, it helps to know that there is someone who cares.

In the midst of the speeches, someone from the Israel Emergency Solidarity Fund, an American organization that has helped Toby in her efforts, asks me if I would be willing to speak to a reporter from CNN. I say yes. I am ready. I feel that I can speak without crying, without breaking down. Speaking on TV doesn't intimidate me after Koby's murder. I walk over to the cameras. A reporter sticks a large microphone into my face and asks me to tell my story. I tell him about Koby, about the way he was killed. He asks if I have any words for the people of America. I tell him that the pain of mourning is so intense that you wish that you could die. It's a pain that you don't think you can bear, but you can bear it. You need to be around people who can live with pain, not people who want you to finish with it, to get it behind you. Pain is like carrying a heavy barbell in your backpack. You can't go as freely as you used to. But the more you carry it, the stronger you get.

The reporter asks me a few more questions and then he puts the microphone down. I look at him closely for the first time. He's wearing jeans, he's balding and his eyes are the turquoise blue of the Dead Sea on a crisp clear day.

"I know you," I say.

"You're right," he says.

"What's your name?" I ask, though I know his name.

He turns to me and his eyes are filled with tears.

"Alon," I say.

"It's been a long time," he says.

Alon Bernstein and I dated eighteen years ago, for a short time. Alon and I sat in East Jerusalem drinking Turkish coffee. We climbed

Masada together. Alon asked me to marry him. I liked him a lot, but not enough to marry him. Still, I considered it. He tells me he has three boys. He wipes a tear away with the sleeve of his denim shirt.

"It's okay," I tell him. "I cry day and night." I know he is sad for me. But I think he is also crying because he knows, if I had married him, it could have been his child who died. He's come that close.

The mayor and some of the dignitaries and others who have sponsored this day go to Sbarro's pizza place in downtown Jerusalem, the site of a suicide bombing five weeks earlier where fifteen adults and children were killed. The pizza place is reopening. My friend Frimet's fifteen-year-old-daughter, Malki, a poet and flute player, was killed there. I can't join them. The place is too painful for me.

Israel has now become a model to America of how to cope with terror. You don't let it stop you; you don't let it interfere; you don't let it dictate your movements. You go on as if life is ordinary. You go on, and in going on, you stand up to evil.

"Now we are all New Yorkers," says the mayor. It's true. But what's also true is this: now we are all Israelis.

I look at Alon. He is packing up, on to the next story. I do not leave this story behind. I carry this death with me, everywhere I go, into every moment of my life. I carry it in a place deep inside of me, where no camera can penetrate.

Chapter thirty-two

Pain and Forgiveness

Recently, we had a two-day Healing Retreat for Mothers. During the art therapy session, one of the mothers drew a bottle of ketchup. She said that her son loved ketchup. He was sixteen and was murdered on the Ben Yehuda mall one Saturday night when he went out to celebrate his friend's birthday. Many of the boys at the party were killed or injured. The mother said she could no longer bring herself to buy ketchup.

Losing a child pervades everything. Everywhere you go you see the loss—in the supermarket, when you are in the street, in your cupboards and in your refrigerator. Your life is stained with loss.

What do you do with the pain?

Zahava Gilmore's twenty-five-year-old son, Aish Kodcsh, was killed by terrorists on October 30, 2000. There is a hike on the anniversary of his death, six months after Koby's murder. As we walk, she says to me: "The pain has changed a lot. I want to take his spirit now, his strength and love and joy, and I want that to fill me. That is my tribute to my son. Not to live in pain, but to live as he did, full of joy."

An Italian TV crew asks me if I can forgive Koby's killers one day. I answer, "I will never forgive. What they did was unforgivable." But I will not live my life in anger; I will not answer hate with hate; rage with rage.

It is not my job to forgive. It is the murderer's job to ask forgiveness. Judaism is not a religion of instant forgiveness. It is a religion of remembering. If a person wants to be forgiven, he needs to ask for forgiveness. But no terrorist has asked for my forgiveness. In fact, I haven't been contacted by any Arab who has wanted to console me. I'm not sure how I would greet him. But Jewish law tells us that a person should ask for forgiveness at least three times until the one he has wronged accepts his apology. If the person he has wronged refuses, he should continue to ask—but the wrongdoer has fulfilled his own repentance.

My job is not to forgive—but to give meaning. My job is to remember.

I will remember that the rock of Jacob, my son Koby's name, is another name for God, and that Jacob put rocks together as a pillow to dream on. A rock can be an instrument of rage or a symbol of God's holiness. Even the name rock can be the name of God. Anything can be exploited for evil, or sanctified for holiness.

My heart is a well that had been stopped up with a stone, like the wells that Abraham dug that later became plugged with stone. "I will remove the heart of stone from their bodies and give them a heart of flesh," says the prophet Ezekiel. Koby's death breaks my heart of stone so that my tears are an endless spring that soaks the ground and allows the seeds planted there to break through the darkness.

Chapter thirty-three

God's Silence

Sometimes God is quiet, too quiet. God's silence in the face of evil is immaculate. I want to grab God and shake Him: I want to hit Him. I want to hurt Him. "How could you let my son be killed so brutally? Why didn't you do something?" I imagine Koby's death as if he were torn apart limb by limb, by wolves, his red blood staining the sparkling snow of the tundra. But it was men who killed my son in the desert.

How could God let my son be killed so brutally? I believe the Talmud when it says that God suffers as we suffer. God is in pain when people are in pain. He may glance away but He knows what is going on. He is looking through the lattice at us, His eyes filled with tears.

Many people give up belief in God because of the suffering they witness. But I refuse to believe in God's cruelty. I believe that what we view as cruelty may one day, in fact, be revealed as part of God's plan.

The relationship between Jacob and Joseph in the book of Genesis demonstrates the way that the truth is obscured in this world.

Joseph, Jacob's son, was thrown into a pit and left by his brothers to die because they were jealous of him. Then Joseph was sold as a slave to the family of Potiphar. Sent to prison, Joseph was able to interpret dreams and rose to the heights of leadership in Egypt. As a result, he was able to help his family when the brothers were forced to go down to Egypt to look for food. Joseph's suffering was part of God's plan to ensure that the Jewish people could survive; yet his father, Jacob, had to endure twenty-two years of suffering, mourning for his son.

After Jacob's death, the brothers were afraid that Joseph would turn on them for the evil they had done to him, throwing him into a pit and selling him as a slave. But Joseph understood that the story was bigger than his personal pain. He told his brothers, "And you, you meant evil against me, but God meant it for good."

I try to believe that my Jacob's story—Koby's story—is also much larger than us, much larger than our suffering. Still it is hard to accept a God who could allow Koby to be killed so brutally.

A *midrash* tells us that God has to control his natural inclination to punish the evil, even though he would like to do so, because if he were to punish evil then man could not freely choose to do good: when people acted wrongly, we would immediately be punished. If we knew we were going to be punished each time we neglected to help a friend, then we would quickly learn to help, no matter how busy we were.

But it seems that God wants us to choose; God wants us to act in the world, and freely choose the good. Because only through human beings acting in the world can the world move towards perfection. God doesn't promise that we won't suffer. The sad truth is that suffering is built into our world. "Can't God find another theme?" I ask a friend. "I'm tired of this one." The pain of living in a world of cruelty is overwhelming. Today, as I write, there is a suicide bombing in Jerusalem, killing ten, almost all of them teenage boys; there is a bus bombing in Haifa with fifteen killed; there is a drive by shooting, killing one. All on the same day. The only way that I can cope is to cry out to God: Help us, God, help us.

It's not bearable. But it is.

God promises us that we will grow in our suffering. "If you will listen to *HaShem*, your God, then I will not strike you with any of the illnesses I placed upon Egypt." By illnesses, God is referring to the plagues before the Jewish exodus from Egypt. Rabbi Simcha Zissel Ziv explains that God doesn't mean he won't strike us with suffering. God means that he will give us an opportunity to learn from our pain, to turn toward God and improve ourselves and the world because of our pain.

It's painful to contemplate God's ability to stand back and let the most abominable evil occur. But Professor Yeshayahu Leibowitz, an Israeli scholar, says that because God doesn't do what you want doesn't mean there's not a God. God's silence does not mean that He is indifferent. God's silence is a voice, like the voice in the wadi, a still hushed voice, a voice that in giving us free choice grants us our own voice—our own way of responding to the world, our own way of coping with the mystery and pain of living. When Jacob, disguised as Esau in his hunter's clothing, asked his father, Isaac, for the blessing meant for Esau, the blessing of the first born, Isaac said to Jacob: "The voice is the voice of Jacob, but the hands are the hands of Esau." What are the hands and what is the voice? The *Sfat Emet*,* tells us that Esau's hands are the hands of physical might. Jacob's voice is the voice of prayer. Prayer is the most intimate expression of our pain at not knowing why we suffer. Prayer is our deepest, most authentic language, a language that cries out for connection, for order, for understanding.

Where once I considered prayer an ancient ritual, now prayer offers me solace. It is the language that speaks to me now. Prayer is the thread that weaves me to God, the needle that pierces God's silence.

---

* Rabbi Yehuda Aryeh Leib, the rabbi of Ger, who lived in Poland in the 19th century

Chapter thirty-four

A Hierarchy of Suffering

There are 903 ways to die, according to the Talmud. The way that Koby died may be the worst way. There are probably 902 easier ways to die. In fact, the Talmud has a discussion of which is the harder death: stoning or fire, and most sages agree that stoning is the most difficult death. In the hierarchy of pain, I am a winner.

Avraham brought his son to be sacrificed, but in the end, Isaac was spared. A Midrash tells us that Sarah died when she heard that Isaac had almost been killed. Her keening is the origin of the wailing sound of the ram's horn, the *shofar*, that is blown on *Yom Kippur* and *Rosh HaShana*, the sound that is supposed to awaken us to repentance.

I also serve that function. I feel that people look at me and love their kids more. When I'm in the supermarket in Efrat, I see how people look at me. I know that now when I walk around, many people look at me and think: thank God I'm not her, thank God I still have my kids, my family intact. Thank God I still have my wholeness. And they're right. Koby's murder is a robbery, an amputation, and a rape. I stand naked, battered. Yet I also stand with my angels, my belief, my openness to life.

Still, the other mothers console themselves by comparing the deaths of their children to Koby's death, which seems more brutal to them. A mother whose daughter was killed in a drive-by shooting near Jerusalem said to me: "I suffer, but not like you. I know my daughter died instantly."

Another mother, whose daughter died of cancer, says: "I suffer, but not like you. I know my daughter died peacefully. I was with her when she died. But you?"

In fact, my friends tell me I'm famous for my pain, famous because of Koby. Few have had a son killed as cruelly as I.

And yet I believe that the minute that Koby saw the hate on his murderers' faces, he went into shock and his soul left him. He went into a safe, protected place in his soul. He watched his death, but he was already with God. He was already being comforted, sheltered.

Rabbi Yitzhak Breitowitz, the rabbi of a congregation in Silver Spring, Maryland, told me that dying because you are Jewish means that you die sanctifying God's name. As a result, your soul goes straight up to God. Usually, according to Jewish sources, the soul undergoes a waiting period, a period of purification before ascending to God. But Koby was pure. In fact, Rabbi Breitowitz told me, the usual procedure of cleansing the body of a dead person was not necessary for Koby and Yosef, since they died as pure souls.

There are different opinions but our tradition tells us that the soul hovers around the body for a year, because the soul misses the body. But not Koby. He was free of his body the moment he died. He was already one of God's beloved, sitting on God's lap. That's why I didn't feel him at his grave the day of his funeral.

And now I am the woman whom people don't know how to address. I fill people with the dread of death. I remind them that death is around us. But by being the person nobody wants to be, I can console others because I am not separate from anybody's pain. I can't distance myself. I don't have that luxury. I can be there for others because my suffering includes so many of the permutations of pain.

Chapter thirty-five

Purim

To look at me, you wouldn't know that in the central core of my being, I am in loss, in pain. You wouldn't know that my oldest child has been viciously killed by terrorists. This Purim, I understand God. I don't mean that egotistically. I understand God because I feel that the deepest part of me is hidden.

How can I tell the truth of my experience? It is like unleashing a volcano. To share the depth of my being requires attention and pain. I can't go there all the time. And I don't want to overwhelm others with the grief at the core of my being. So recently, on a few occasions, I have disguised my identity so as not to be forced to reveal the truth inside of me.

Concealing the truth is sometimes thought of as a kind of lie. Before this, I was the kind of person who never lied. I felt that honesty was truth and that I needed to engage in truth, at all costs. I had a teenager's anathema for hypocrisy.

Yet now I find that my thinking was naïve. I understand now that lying is not necessarily dishonest. God himself did not totally disclose the truth so as not to offend Avraham. When an angel told

Sarah that she would have a baby, she laughed to herself, telling the angel she was no longer 'in the way of women', and that her 'husband was too old'. When God, however, recounted the conversation to Avraham he said that Sarah had laughed because she said she was too old. This is taken as an example of God keeping peace in the house. Occasionally concealing my identity is a way of maintaining a sense of peace within myself.

I don't want others to feel for me all the time. I don't want to be related to as a bereaved mother every second of every minute of my life.

I have greater insight now about the issue of concealment. God has to conceal himself to offer us a deeper truth. If he were to reveal his light at all times, we couldn't live with it. It would be too overwhelming.

The motif of concealment is central to the Purim story. On Purim, the name of God is not mentioned in the Megillah. And traditionally we wear masks to conceal our true identities. On Purim we learn that evil is a temporary concealment of good. The symbol of evil, Haman, and the symbol of good, Mordechai, are interchangeable. The evaluations we give to the events in the story become meaningless, because God tells us that good and evil are one and the same, in some deep way. In other words, the true nature of the world is usually concealed from us.

I must acknowledge that I have a lot of trouble with that concept. Having your son stoned to death brutally by Palestinian terrorists doesn't seem like the kind of thing to which one can say: "*Gam zu le'tovah*" ("This, too, is for the good").

Yesterday, eight months after his big brother Koby was killed, my six-year-old son said to me: "Mommy if everything God does is for the good, how can Koby being dead be good?"

He got it, right to the heart of the problem.

I told him that it's not good for us, but maybe it's good for the world, maybe they needed a great kid like Koby to die, so good things could come out of it. For example, parents have told me that they've become better parents from hearing my story.

I will never say that my son's death is good. I miss him and mourn him too much. But I don't want to carry death like the dead bird that last week caught on the hood of my car, thumping up and down, in and out of my vision, a symbol of pain and captivity. I want to carry death as an awareness of a bird that is free, soaring beyond the horizon of what I can see.

The only way I can do that is to believe in my incapacity to know. I have to believe that God has a plan, even if this plan hurts us. Yesterday I saw a glimpse of God's plan. I rode on the bus with a woman from my town, Rivka El Nekave, the secretary at the school my younger children attend. Her father left Afghanistan fifty years ago on horseback to come to Israel. Rivka is stunningly beautiful; her face seems lit from within. She was the adult in charge on the school trip with my son, Daniel, the day that Koby was murdered. The teacher was gone, and Rivka was left to supervise. She was the one who had to tell Daniel and the other children the awful news, and to comfort the children.

I learned that she is intimately acquainted with loss. She told me that her mother had died giving birth to her thirty-five years ago. She grew up as an only child, motherless. Her father remarried, and she didn't get along with her stepmother. She was the person who could tell Daniel with compassion and understanding. She was the one who had the capacity to contain the pain, and was able to comfort and help the children, maybe even to help her heal herself.

Sometimes we are formed more by what we are missing than by what we are given. Our courage and our compassion are built from pain.

And if that is the case, then to say—"This, too, is for the good"—even to the evil and pain of suffering in our life, is a truer way to live. The pain we feel is extraordinarily powerful and over-whelming. But the pain can either push a person into a spiral of depression or be an impetus and a spur for growth. It depends on how we handle it.

On Purim, we drink so that we can see the deepest truths in the world—even the murderous advisor to King Ahaseurus, Haman, who wanted to see all the Jews in the kingdom killed, can be seen for the *tov*, the good. We acknowledge that some truths are beyond the measures of our minds, which are confined to polarity. Some truths are beyond the confines of language, where words limit and skew, rather than reveal. Some truths are best borne in silence, which is the true language of concealment.

Perhaps our very bodies are disguises for the soul within, and we make the choice, to allow the language of the soul to speak in the world, or to keep the soul imprisoned like a dead bird thumping against our windshield.

"There is no rung of being on which we cannot find the holiness of God everywhere and at all times," say the Chassidic masters. (Martin Buber, *Ten Rungs*)

It's hiding. But it's there. We have to keep looking.

Koby with his two grandmothers

Chapter thirty-six

My Grandmother's Mantra

Koby's death makes me reevaluate everything, even my grandmother's mantra. I first learned about my mantra in 1966 when I was in fifth grade and was the spokesperson for my group in a debate on Vietnam for my social studies class. The debate took place in the auditorium in front of the whole elementary school. Even though I was a good student, current events were not my strength. I don't come from one of those families that discussed the news of the day at the dining room table. I wasn't allowed to write anything in advance and when my turn came to sum up Lyndon Johnson and the Democrat's point of view on the war, I couldn't keep North and South Vietnam straight. I couldn't remember whose side we were on. I mumbled something, but I had no idea what I was talking about.

When I got home, I was too embarrassed to tell my mother about what had happened. I kept crying. She said: Just take a deep breath. Then she said: You need to relax and then she said—"Do what my mother told me to do, take this word and say it over and over until it calms you. Just think about that word and forget everything else." She rubbed my temples and I lay down and said the word and it filled my mind and calmed me.

My mother told me her mother had given it to her when my mother, aged fifteen at the time, had her first job at a health clinic during World War II. When the soldiers came back, she was fired, and by accident she pressed all of the buttons on the files, locking them shut. For some reason, there was no key. The boss yelled at her and told her she was a fool. My mother came home sobbing. Her mother gave her the mantra to keep her calm.

It wasn't until 1973, before my first day of college that I thought of my mantra again. My parents had dropped me off at my dorm room at Mary Donlon Hall, and I was scared and lonely and in a panic. When I went to sleep that first night, I said the mantra to myself.

The next time my mother and I discussed the mantra, it was 1995. I was forty years old; a mother of four and my father was dying of cancer in his home. I'd just made aliyah six months earlier. Now I'd flown in to be with my parents in Florida. My mother and I were having trouble sleeping because we were so worried about my father who had stopped eating and was hooked up to a feeding tube.

I woke up cold in the middle of the night. I walked into the kitchen. My mother sat at the kitchen table in a pink silk bathrobe. We could hear my father coughing in his sleep. We drank tea with milk and I said: "We need our mantra."

She said, "You're right." She began to murmur: "Belladonna, belladonna." (I can't tell you the real name because a mantra must remain a secret.)

"What are you saying?" I asked.

She said, "The mantra. Grandma's mantra."

I said, "Ma, that's the name of a poison. That's not our mantra."

"Are you sure?" she asked.

"Yes, our mantra's a plant. But it's not a poison. How could Grandma have given us the name of a poison to say? You forgot what it was."

"What is it?" she asked.

So I told her our mantra. Lavender (also not the real one...) She was so upset, she'd forgotten it. Luckily, she'd given it to me. Now I could give it back to her. We closed our eyes and recited it, and soon we relaxed a bit and went back to our beds.

A few weeks later, I talked to my older sister and asked her if my mother had ever given her a mantra. She said yes. And then I asked her what it was. She said, "Belladonna."

I was the one who'd been saying the wrong mantra.

But as I thought about it, I realized that my own mantra was the right one, the right one for me. I couldn't say the name of a poison. It just wouldn't work for me. I took what I'd been given and transformed it into something I could love, something that spoke to my soul. Lavender.

I thought I had shaped my mantra with my own inner voice.

But now that Koby has been murdered, I can't say lavender anymore. I realize: the mantra that was passed down to me, the poison, that is the right mantra. I can't chant a word that doesn't have an underbelly of violence and horror. I can't say a word that doesn't tie beauty to pain. I need to say a word that is in itself a contradiction—something to calm me with its poison.

And something else truly startling occurred. As I kept saying the mantra, I realized that the mantra I'd been given—a word in English—had a depth I had never even considered. For when I kept saying this word, I found the words inside of my word. And inside the word was a Hebrew word, the word, He is my God. So by giving me this mantra, my grandmother had chosen wisely. I have no idea where she got her mantra. I can't imagine my Hungarian great grandmother giving her one. But it is possible. After all, my grandmother had a baby die at the age of a week. He was never named. Uncle Baby we called my uncle, whose gravestone we visited on our infrequent visits to the cemetery in New Jersey.

Perhaps this mantra is his name and the name of all that die young—an admission that God is full of pain and beauty and mystery, and that they are all joined in God's name, like the foul smelling fragrance—the galbanum—in the incense that the high priest brings to the temple. Without that necessary ingredient, that malodorous substance, the combination of fragrances in the incense would not smell as sweet.

Chapter thirty-seven

Humility

Moses was a humble person. When God chose him to bring the Jews out of Egypt, he protested that there were other, more suitable people to transmit the word of God. Moses stuttered and did not think he could speak. But God insisted. One of the reasons that God chose Moses was his humility. Moses was able to listen and to transmit God's word as God had spoken it, without a spin, without editorial, without adding his interpretation. His humility gave him a clarity that allowed him to encounter the fullness of God's expression.

When Moses asked to see God's glory, God told him that He would put him in a crevice of the mountain, protecting him with his hand until he passed through. Then he removed his hand, and Moses had a vision of God. Moses saw God from behind. But the vision was the back of God, not his face.

The Warsaw Ghetto rabbi, Kolonymos Kalman Shapira, tells us that even when we experience God's hiddenness, we should not think we are really hidden from God's hands, because we are carved there like God's palms. "Behold I have carved you upon the palms of my hands," (Isaiah 49:16) (*Sacred Fire*, Rabbi Kalonymous Shapira). It is, he says, "the ultimate closeness" and asserts that a person can be "strong and upstanding" even at a time of hiddenness.

It is as if God is playing a game of Hide-and-Seek: cover your eyes when I am close because the glory will be too overwhelming; when you uncover them, I will be gone, you will not be able to find me face on, but you will know that I was there.

I know you were here.

God Himself is humble. He dwells in humility. The Messiah himself is a humble beggar because only one who has experienced desperate need can empty himself to feel the compassion and kindness needed in this world, and extend that love to all of humanity.

Rabbi Dov Baer of Mezritch, a disciple of the Baal Shem Tov (Israel ben Eliezer, the eighteenth century founder of Hasidism) taught that a "person needs to regard himself as if he were nothing. Forget yourself in every way…Only then will you be able to attain the ultimate preparation—which is the same as the world of consciousness, for there, everything is equal, life and death, sea and dry land."

Yet we are created to be in relationship with God, to be full partners. Every person is obligated to say, "The world was created for me." (*Sanhedrin* 37a) So we also must think well of ourselves, recognize the divinity within us.

We must be full and empty at the same time. Death, if you let it, teaches you how to do this.

A friend who is caring for a child who is an invalid and mentally impaired tells me: Your love for Koby is a deeper love because you don't get anything from him. You still have a relationship. You have a relationship with his soul. Your love is less selfish because you are the one who keeps giving.

She's wrong about not getting anything from him. I do get something from him. I am full and empty. I lose the love, the joy, the security of an intact life. But I learn the beauty of surrender, I gain each moment, the ability to enter the moment because I want to value each moment given to me, for me and for Koby.

Humility means that I recognize that one day even grieving

will assume its proper proportion. In time, I will learn to give death its measure, and no more. Koby is more present in my life now than he has ever been. Not an hour goes by that he is not in my head and heart. Every morning I rise to his death and every evening I go to sleep with it. The trick is to forbid death to be more present than life, not to forsake my life and my other children for the memory of all that I have lost. I need to focus my love and attention on my children and husband who are here with me.

Humility can help me do that, let go of the pain.

The Jewish calendar can help me do so. Koby died during the seven-week period between Passover and Shavuot, the period of the *Omer* (meaning a measurement or small quantity). This period between the time of harvest and the first fruits is a period of vulnerability and anxiety because it is during this period that our quantity of food for the whole year is determined. It is also a time of calamity in Jewish history. Fourteen thousand of Rabbi Akiva's students were struck with a plague during the Omer. Even today, it is a period of mourning for the Jewish people. It is customary to observe certain mourning practices during this time, for example haircuts and weddings are not permitted until after Shavuot. An exception is made on the day of *Lag b'Omer*, the thirty-third day of the forty-nine-day period of the Omer, since this day (when the plague ceased and the students of Rabbi Akiva stopped dying) is considered a joyous time.

Our tragedy occurred on the thirtieth day of the *Omer* count. Each week of this count in the Jewish tradition corresponds to an emotional quality. The week that Koby died was the week of *hod*, which means splendor. Kabbalists associate the word *hod* with the words to thank, to acknowledge, or to admit. *Hod* indicates the ability to surrender to God, to humble oneself in the face of God's greatness and His plan. Humility is not a passive quality. Humility requires strength, an ability to stand before God's greatness and surrender to it, not out of weakness but out of respect, recognition, and awe of all that God is. Sometimes humility is like light moving through a projector. The light first has to be condensed in the darkness before it can be projected. Only then can we see the image, the story, the meaning.

When Rabbi Chaim Brovender spoke to bereaved parents at a family healing retreat run by our Foundation, he said that our experiences were hard to communicate. We had experienced the traumatic deaths of our children, but these deaths were also part of Jewish history, connecting us to the sweep of history. As such, the death of our children and our experiences had a kind of grandeur to them.

Perhaps the strength of humility is the ability to bow to the grandeur of what we have experienced—to be humble enough to see the majesty of God's power in our lives, to be humble enough to see beyond our tears.

Chapter thirty-eight

Heaven

My fifteen-year-old friend, Ma'ayan, tells me that she met a sixteen-year-old guy at the Jerusalem Mall after Koby was murdered. He didn't know Koby. But when she told him that she was Koby's friend, he said, "Don't worry about him. He went straight to heaven. And there you have all the weed you want. It's great stuff. And you don't even have to light it."

"What's hell?" she asked him.

"Hell is dope everywhere, all over, but there's no way to light it."

I consider this young boy's explanation of heaven and hell. Only a sixteen-year-old could be that original. And suddenly I realize: maybe being young when you die is an advantage. Because there are so many people in heaven who are old and tired, who took eighty years to complete their tasks on earth. Maybe it's good to be young.

I think of Koby up there, with all of his energy, his vitality, still eager to go on, to learn, to create. Maybe he is building a house up there, for all of the old souls to live in. Maybe he is making me a room, so that when I die, I'll have a place up there where I can feel comfortable, a place I will recognize as my own.

I know that Koby is very busy up in heaven. But he has also been working very hard creating possibilities and sending messages to us down here. For example, Koby's hero, the baseball player Cal Ripken, read our story in the *Baltimore Jewish Times* and contacted us through his agent because he wants to be involved, wants to build a baseball stadium in Israel in Koby's honor. Since that initial contact, we haven't heard from Cal. But somehow, I won't be surprised if we hear from him because Koby would love to have a baseball stadium built in Israel.

Faye Kellerman, one of Koby's favorite writers, turned out to be the hostess when my husband was invited for lunch during his *Shabbat* visit in Los Angeles. There is a bill pending in Congress, the Koby Mandell Act, designed to facilitate justice for Americans killed by Palestinian terrorists.

Most important is our work with the Koby Mandell Foundation. We run several healing programs, which include different retreats for mothers, for whole families, and a camp for some four hundred children, all of whom have lost family members to terror. (See the chapter on the Foundation, page 203)

Last summer, an eleven-year-old girl at the camp whose father had been murdered told the camp mother a recurring dream she hadn't told anybody else. Her father, dressed in flowing white clothes, kept coming to her in a garden but when she ran to him to hug him, he would turn and walk away. But at the camp she had a dream—she saw her father in the garden and when she ran to him, this time, he turned to her and held her and hugged her and told her that she and her mother and the other children would be okay. He was watching over them.

That story of healing is a little bit of heaven for me.

I've mentioned Zahava Gilmore's son, Aish Kodesh Gilmore, who was murdered by terrorists at the age of twenty-five, while working as a guard at a social security office in East Jerusalem. Aish Kodesh's seven-year-old brother told Zahava that, even now, he continues to see Aish Kodesh. He sees him in his heart. To me, that's the best definition of heaven—the place where you see with your heart.

Chapter thirty-nine

The Deer

The day Koby died a deer came out of the canyon, her hooves covered with blood. But there was another deer I'd seen earlier that week... I was driving with my friend Shulamith, a therapist, when suddenly a deer leapt across the road, right in front of us. Shulamith asked me: What does the deer mean to you? I said: "Anything can change in a minute." I thought it was a sign that my life would improve, especially our finances.

Now I know that the deer meant more. The doe is a symbol of the *shechina*, God's female presence in the world. According to Jewish mysticism, no animal in the world feels more empathy. The doe gathers food and feeds others. When the world needs rain, she gathers all the animals around her and leads them to the top of a high mountain, wraps her head between her knees and wails for God to provide rain. (*Zohar, Pinchas* 249a) She is the ultimate symbol of heavenly compassion.

The *Zohar* relates a parable in which a doe has difficulty giving birth; she puts her head between her knees and suffers the anguish of giving birth, but is unable to push the fawn out. Her womb is too narrow. But at the precise moment at which she writhes in suffering and agony, a snake comes and bites her. The pain causes the opening to widen. Only then is she able to give birth. It is the snake, the evil, that creates the pain that opens her to birth. It is only through the partnership of the compassionate deer, and the malevolent snake, that birth can proceed. This is the way that the birth of the redemption, the birth of the Messiah, will unfold.

This story contains the secret of the mystery of evil in the universe. Each encounter with evil moves us closer to the birth of the Messiah and the coming of the redemption. According to Jewish mysticism, the amount of evil in the world is limited, fixed at the creation of the universe, when God constricted his light to create a space for creation. The vessels that he poured his light into could not hold the radiance and shattered. Most of the light returned to its source, to God. Some of the light, however, was absorbed into the walls of the vessels and became trapped there. This light is in exile, and our task as human beings is to redeem that light, to bring goodness into the world, and raise that light to heaven.

Yet it seems that evil is exploding, growing larger and fiercer each day. But each confrontation with evil has the possibility of recapturing the light that was spilled and hidden in the world. Evil will one day be eradicated, if we allow it to be.

Each day, the world can move closer to healing itself. Elijah and Moses and Shimon Bar Yochai are all expressions of God's presence in the world. All hid in caves; all received God's holy light when they fled to the cave for protection. Only when they entered the cave, the greatest darkness, and dwelt there, were they able to reveal the light of holiness and God to the world. In the blessing we recite before the *Shema*, we bless God who forms light and creates darkness. It is the darkness that gives us the ability to bless the light.

"I saw that light gained an additional luster from darkness" (Ecclesiastes 2:13) In each of us there is a spark of Elijah trying to emerge from the darkness and bring healing to the world.

One morning recently, I woke so early that the sky looked like it was on fire. I realized that the intense glory of the light is only gained after being submerged in the darkness of a long night, when the sky is shattered by the rising sun. Only then is the radiance of the light revealed in its most intense purity.

Seeing the spark of light in the darkness may be the very definition of faith. My darkness is part of the suffering of our whole nation—which so far has lost over seven hundred precious people to terrorist attacks (to say nothing of the thousands injured), part of the birth pangs of the Messiah. The process of Redemption is the process of God giving birth.

Koby and Yosef's death is the snake biting the deer. We are meant to be moved to give birth, to faith and strength. The biblical Rachel, dying in childbirth, calls her son Binyamin, Ben *oni*, 'the son of my sorrow.' But Binyamin's father, Jacob, referred to the infant as: 'the son of my strength.' The word *oni* in Hebrew means both pain and strength. "It is the very nature of holiness to translate pain into strength—even to intuit the strength within the pain, the coherence within chaos," says Torah scholar Avivah Zornberg in *Genesis: The Beginning of Desire*.

Holiness means clinging to strength, clinging to wholeness and healing.

Chapter forty

Our Wedding Anniversary

Ｗe are not much, usually, for celebrating our anniversary on May 28, primarily because our anniversary has always coincided with the birth of our son, Daniel, on the same day. My son was my anniversary present. I needed no other. When Daniel was little I was always so exhausted by his birthday parties that I had no energy to honor my own celebration of marriage. But May 28, 2002, was different. We'd already given Daniel his *Bar Mitzvah*, and since he had been deluged with love and attention—not to mention presents—we didn't need to mark his birthday. Instead we went out to lunch, just my husband and me.

When we walked into the restaurant, a waitress greeted us with an enormous smile, telling me that she liked my skirt. This young woman with her dark black, shiny hair had a spirit and effervescence I could only admire. I thought to myself: she has no idea of the pain I am living with, the weight of what I carry. Thank God she has no idea of the suffering that can be part of life, the way that every happiness that I experience now is infused with loss. Thank God she is innocent of that.

187

As my husband and I ate our meal, we realized that the restaurant was a perfect place to commemorate what would be Koby's upcoming fifteenth birthday. We wanted to take fifteen poor or disadvantaged people out to dinner to mark Koby's birthday—to add joy to the living.

We spoke to the manager about our plans. He said that he volunteered at a nearby center that helped disadvantaged teens from poor, broken families and he thought the teenagers would appreciate going out with us. The idea was materializing almost on its own. We hadn't thought about taking teens for a meal, but it made sense. After all, Koby was a teen when he was killed. We felt that up above, Koby was pulling some strings to help us organize his birthday. When we told the manager that Koby's birthday was on a Friday, he said that they normally didn't serve lunch on Fridays, but he would open the restaurant especially for our group.

We thanked him and before he walked away, my husband said: "Do you know the Goodman family? They live around here. They lost their son this year in an accident—we went to the *shiva*—and I wanted to know how they were doing."

"You can ask them yourself. Your waitress is their daughter."

I looked at her, at her beauty and her spirit, and I thought— you never know what's going on inside a person. I had so misjudged her. She came over to the table, and we told her of our loss and she shared her own. I felt like we were sisters of the soul. I told her what I had thought when I first saw her—how untouched she was by pain, how innocent. We talked about the pain of living with death; how it's a weight that can crush you or make you stronger, depending on how you carry it. We told her how wonderful it was to have her as our waitress on this day, since we had been fearful of celebrating our anniversary.

As we spoke, I realized how much of life is hidden. We don't see what's inside of people. Inside of almost everybody is a pocket of pain—some pockets are bigger, some are smaller—but they are always there. We can't see somebody else's heartache until they share it with us. I find that when I don't share my pain, it is like an unwanted guest at the table, somebody who demands fancy china, ironed napkins; a guest with whom I can never feel comfortable. But when I share the pain, it becomes somebody I can live with. Somebody who will sit at the table with me in pajamas. I don't have to stand on ceremony with it.

Which is the way Yael, the waitress, treated us. Suddenly we looked up to see her carrying a piece of cake with a sputtering sparkler candle in the middle.

"Happy anniversary," she said to us with a huge smile on her face.

I can't help but feel that Koby arranged this gathering and gave us this present. I can't help but feel that if I could see more clearly, I would see God and Koby and Yael's brother, Tani, somewhere above, lighting the candles.

Chapter forty-one

Not Knowing

I will not choose despair. I need to choose miracles. I need to keep breathing. As Rabbi Soloveitchik says: "Faith begins where human reason ends."

I believe. Until. A wave crashes against me and I get pounded along the bottom of the ocean. My faith breaks down and I am pulverized like my son's body. But then I begin again.

The divided heart lives with contradiction. A friend once said to me: our children are our teachers. In death, Koby is teaching me more than I have learned from anyone alive. His death has taught me how little we know about even our own children. For a child is different outside of the house, he shows another face to the world. The day after Koby died, his friends came to our house and asked if they could go into his room. Seth told them to come back the next day. He thought they knew Koby had something secreted away that they wanted to get out of the house. Seth wanted to know what it was.

But when he looked through his drawers, he found his own prayer book. He looked inside of Koby's wallet. There was the blessing to say after eating. Inside of his drawers Seth found books of psalms, and the Torah. Under his bed were baseball cards and a candle. What surprised Seth was that instead of the compromising magazine or cigarettes he expected to find, Koby had been hiding prayers and books of holiness.

I learned about Koby after he died. The person I thought I knew best in the world was different in the outside world. There he was more generous, more compassionate.

One boy from his class whom we didn't know came to us at the *shiva*. The other boys from Koby's class pushed him toward us and told us he had something important to tell us. He was short, stooped over and wore glasses. He stood next to us for a moment. Then he spoke so quietly we could hardly hear him. He said that Koby was the best athlete in the class, while he was the worst. One day in gym class, they were playing volleyball, and the teacher asked them to get into pairs.

"Koby had first choice," he said, "and Koby picked me. Koby wanted to teach me."

I was amazed to hear this. Koby who was all power and might, and the most competitive kid you can imagine—Koby would only root for the winner when we watched sports on TV. When his team started losing, he'd simply change teams. He loved the Bulls with Michael Jordan but changed his allegiance immediately after Michael Jordan's departure. He wanted to be with the winners. And yet, when it was needed, he was a boy with tremendous compassion.

We will take Koby's compassion and plant it in the world, so that it can keep growing.

Chapter forty-two

Passover 2002

K oby loved Passover. He would learn for the *Seder* night and then eagerly engage in the conversation about the *Haggadah*. Ask any grieving person and they will tell you that the holidays are like a knife in the most tender part of the heart. When the whole family is together, the ache of longing and of memories is most acute.

Yet I find pleasure in Passover, even now. Living in Israel means that as I prepare for Passover I feel that I am not alone. I am preparing with the whole country as we clean out the *chametz*, the leavened material, from our houses and, also, from our souls. The food stores change their shelves, their wares, and you can see people carting trash at all hours of the day and night. There is the feeling of upheaval. Of transformation. People are shedding their skins and starting anew. We all try to begin again. We are trying to be as humble as the simple *matzah*, with no filling. We are trying to become our best selves—our insides and outside congruous.

The Torah tells us that the month of Passover, Nissan, the time when the people of Israel were released from their servitude, should be counted as the first of months. *Chodesh*, the word for month, has the same root as the Hebrew word *chadash*, which means 'new'. Each month we have the opportunity for growth, for change, for renewal—like the moon. We can become better, more giving, more generous, more loving. We can leave the confines of our narrow vision. Nissan, the month of our redemption, can be a month of budding new life. But before that growth can occur we need to clean out. It's surprising that the preparation for a holiday about freedom centers around cleaning. But as I clean, I understand that cleaning is about going behind and under, going into what is usually hidden and dark to expose the underbelly of our surroundings. It's about appreciating and elevating the mundane. We see what we don't usually see. It is the first step toward change—a deep consciousness of what is, the situation in which we find ourselves.

Grief also makes you pay attention to what you normally don't see. When you are grieving, you see what is usually in shadow—the darkness under the bed, the cobwebs on the ceiling, the shadows that make us afraid and remind us that we too will die. Many psychologists are in agreement: it is only when a grieving person faces his or her pain, that he or she can begin the slow process of healing.

Here in Israel, we are living through a time of what feels like Biblical suffering. Whether we sit at home or drive on the road or go to a cafe, we are targets for terror. Missing my son has forced me to be intimate with evil and horror, to lift the rock under which the maggots lie.

On the first night of Passover, *Seder* night, we make a blessing on the bitter herb. In blessing the bitter, we say that even the bitter can be redeemed. The Sefat Emet states that eating the *maror*, the bitter, demonstrates our belief that bitterness is only a prelude to liberation. God is with us both in our suffering and in our freedom.

It is as if in Israel today we keep encountering that which is bitter. If we don't become enslaved to our pain, that bitterness can lead us toward redemption.

Chapter forty-three
Jacob's Ladder

My son Daniel designed his brother's gravestone. He wanted Jacob's ladder carved on the gravestone. On this ladder the angels are said to ascend and descend between heaven and the earth, bridging the two worlds. Engraved on Koby's stone is this passage from the Torah: "He dreamed and behold a ladder was set earthward, its top reached to heaven and behold angels of God were ascending and descending on it (Genesis 28:12)."

It's curious that the angels have to ascend first. It seems that they should need to descend from heaven first. Some commentators explain that the rungs are the rungs of the Jewish exile from Israel—the Babylonian, Persian, Greek, and Roman conquests, and the angels are the guardian angels of the conquering nations. But I prefer the opinion of the Rambam. He believes that the angels' ascent means that human beings climb a spiritual ladder. I think we have to climb up ourselves, make ourselves into angels, in order for the angels to come down and meet us.

The angels do descend to give us messages, of that I am sure.

But sometimes the ladder is not so much up and down but between us. The rungs between us become links in a chain.

I felt that sense of connectedness last spring in Jerusalem. A young woman, Michal Franklin, was killed at a bus stop in French Hill. She didn't ordinarily get off the bus there but she wanted to wait with her friend. Michal had finished teacher's seminary that day. The family was ready to celebrate.

But instead a Palestinian suicide bomber got out of a car, ran to the crowded bus stop and blew himself up in front of her. She was killed instantly and the family had to use dental records to identify her. Instead of graduating, she was buried.

When I heard about the deaths, I felt the mothers' pain. You enter a world of pain so thick that you cannot see. You cannot eat or think. You just try to hold on, pummeled by tidal waves and shocks of pain.

That Friday there was a story in the newspaper about Michal Franklin. Later in the day, right before the Sabbath, I was in the bathtub and I had a nagging feeling that there was something I had to complete before the Sabbath. I thought—"What didn't I do this week? What is there left to do?"

And suddenly I realized that I had to tell the Franklins how to make it through *Shabbat*.

I called Sara Franklin to pass along what Ruthie Gillis had told me—how the Sabbath after her husband was murdered by terrorists had been the highest of her life, because of the strength of the people who celebrated the Sabbath with singing and spirit in the face of death. I told Sara how my first Sabbath after Koby's death had been otherworldly, but beautiful. How Ruthie's words had given me permission to allow the power of *Shabbat* to enter me. How I felt like I had crossed into the World-to-Come; how the singing and celebration had come from a place where pain merged with beauty and where eternity seemed to be whispering to me that Koby would never leave me, just like the Sabbath has never left the Jewish people, but returns each week to give us sustenance.

I told her how I hadn't believed Ruthie Gillis, but the glory of *Shabbat* had spoken to me as well.

Sara could hardly speak but she thanked me for calling. I had no idea how my message was received. But the next week, my friend Malka called me. It turns out that she knew the family and they wanted to see me.

When I walked into the house of mourning, Malka introduced me. The father, Avner Franklin, told me that his wife had immediately told him what I had said and that he had called the Jungries family whose teenage daughter had been killed with Michal and told them as well. And now, the father thanked me for transforming their *Shabbat*. He said that they had entered *Shabbat* in a different spirit because of my phone call.

The grandmother was there, a lovely looking woman with an upturned nose and white hair swept into a knot. She said to me that the singing had been beautiful, how the *Shabbat* had had a different quality because of my call.

Then she said: "I don't think Avner understands yet how the pain doesn't leave."

As she raised her arm, I saw a number from the Holocaust branded on her wrist.

Malka later told me that the grandmother had been in Auschwitz and lost her whole family. When she finally had her own family, she had no relative to call when she had her first baby because they'd all been killed. And now her granddaughter. More than fifty years later.

How can we understand this? Where is the ladder that took her pain to heaven and returned it as blessing, only blessing? Where are the angels of God descending to answer our prayers?

There is no answer. But a Chassidic story about the Baal Shem Tov may illuminate a response. The Baal Shem Tov used to take many hours to pray. Many of his followers would leave because they were hungry or tired, but some would remain until the Baal Shem was finished with his prayers. One day all of his followers left him alone and that day he finished very quickly. When they returned they asked him, "How did you finish so quickly?" In response, he related a parable.

"One day there were many people near a tree but only one person could see the beautiful bird in the tree. In order to touch that bird, the man had to stand each person one on top of the other's shoulders, and only then could he reach the bird's nest.

The same is true with prayer. When I stand in prayer, all the worlds open up, even the world of the supernal bird's nest where Messiah waits. But when you leave, I fall from the ladder, and after that there is nothing more for me to do. There is no way I can reach the bird's nest by myself. And so I finished my prayer."

We can't reach our destiny alone. We need to stand on each other's shoulders to give each other strength. In order to climb a ladder, you have to stretch yourself. You have to extend your powers. Only when we are strong enough to hold each other can we enter a place of holiness. Perhaps the Messiah is waiting, until he sees us, carrying each other on our shoulders.

Chapter forty-four

Another Shimon Bar Yochai Story

Afriend calls to tell me how upset she is because she caught her son with a joint. "Great," I say. "What a great problem." She laughs. "You're right," she says. Not that I am for teenagers doing drugs. But still, it is a problem you can work on. Suffering gives you clarity if you allow it to. A child's death gives you a mission in this world. The pain will reveal what you need to learn, the work you need to do.

Suffering lends perspective. Again I understand Rabbi Shimon Bar Yochai from another story about him. One of his students left Israel and went to a foreign country and became very rich. All of his students then decided that they wanted to join the other student. Rabbi Shimon Bar Yochai took them to a valley near Meron and said: "Valley, valley, fill yourself up with gold!"

The valley began to produce gold. "If gold is all you want, here is enough to satisfy all of your desires. Take all of the gold you want, but know: whatever you take now is part of the share you will receive in the World-to-Come. Therefore, there you will receive less. The reward of studying Torah, on the other hand, cannot be received in this world but only in the World-to-Come." The students took none of the gold but returned to their studies. A *midrash* describes the World-to-Come as this: Six hundred thousand angels minister to those who are worthy, removing the garments worn in the grave. Then they dress the worthy in crowns and eight garments made from the clouds of glory. Angels lead them to a place where four rivers flow: one with milk, another with wine, another with persimmon, and the fourth with honey. (*Yalkut Shimoni Genesis*, 20)

But I want this world with Koby in it. I want to take him for braces and watch him get acne. I want to see him struggle with school. I want to hear his voice change. I want to watch him get a moustache. I don't want the World-to-Come. I want him back, beating me at Boggle, playing Scrabble with me as if it were the championship tournament, always trying to use his favorite Scrabble word—zax.

Seth and me. We are learning. All the gold in the world means nothing to us.

When I feel the despair of losing him, I remember my dream: Koby races into the house, smiling, in a mad rush. "I have a soccer camp I have to go to," he says. "I've got to change." And in my dream I'm so happy to see his beautiful face. And I realize that he has come back because he needs to learn soccer. In my dream I realize: We come to this earth to learn something.

Chapter forty-five

The Koby Mandell
Foundation

Everything, even Koby's death, has a purpose. Recently I
had an experience that reinforced my belief in God's plan. I was
invited to Switzerland for a peace conference. Before the trip I had a
dream—my sister and I were in a taxi being driven around a Euro-
pean city, the driver was making sure that we saw the sites—the lake,
the harbor, the museum. Then we realized that our train was leaving.
The driver speeded to the station and let us off. We didn't know how
we would find our train on time. We were very nervous and started
to run. Suddenly, a man greeted us and told us he was there to show
us our train. My sister started complaining that she had a splinter
under her nail and that her nail was hurting her. I said: "How can
you complain about your nail? Look at this. We are being guided,
someone is caring for us, taking us from place to place and you're
complaining about your nail."

A few days later, I traveled to Switzerland. I had to change
planes in Zurich. Before getting off the plane, I asked the man sit-

ting next to me, whom I hadn't spoken to the whole trip, if he knew where I needed to go to get the plane to Geneva. We got up; he took my bag and silently guided me through the airport, wheeling my suitcase for me, leading me for ten minutes until he located my boarding gate.

I don't know his name but I do know that he is part of some greater plan.

Seth and I know that we have to do something to keep Koby's spirit alive. We cannot let his spirit die. As a former Hillel director, Seth has experience running programs and raising money. Many people know about Koby's death; we want to channel the power of the boys' death and we have the ability to do so. We decide to do something that Koby would enjoy; we decide to make a summer camp for the children in Israel whose mothers and fathers and sisters and brothers have been killed by terror. We see that our own kids aren't understood. They go right back to school, and people think they're okay because they play and they seem happy. But inside we know they suffer, they're in pain. Daniel tells us he can't concentrate because he's thinking of Koby. Eliana tells me that when she apologized to a girl in her class for speaking a bit rudely to her, Eliana said: I'm stressed because I miss my brother." The girl, who barely knew Koby, said: "Well that's no reason to be mean to me. I miss him too." The other kids don't understand how much it hurts. So we make a camp where the kids are understood. Our camp director, Reuven Angstreich, runs a wonderful six-week camp. Over four hundred kids join us, and they are happy to be together. We have sports and trips and art and music and movement therapy, but the real pleasure is for the kids not to be alone. Eliana makes friends with a girl, Shir, whose teenage brother had an Internet romance. When he arranged to meet the girl, she turned out to be an Arab woman who lured him into an Arab town where he was shot. Shir can tell Eliana her story because Eliana has a matching atrocity. They can share and understand. They can be happy together because they know that they're in the same situation. They don't feel guilty when they're happy.

One teenage boy tells Seth that he cut his hair because he looked like his brother who was murdered and he could feel his mother shudder sometimes when she saw him. He knew he reminded his mother of the beloved dead son. He couldn't tell his mother this. But in camp, the kids express things they can't say in the family where they don't want to hurt their parents more than they've already been hurt.

During the year after Koby's murder, as the terror attacks continue, if there is an American family involved (because I'm still simply more comfortable expressing deep feelings in English) I often phone or make a *shiva* call. And after I do, I tell Shira about the family, and I say I think you should call them. She does and slowly we start an informal support network. I see that it helps me to give and to be part of other people's stories. I know what to say to them. Yosef's mother, Rena Ish-Ran, one day tells me how much she needs some time to herself, time away from her kids and husband, time only for her. And I think how wonderful it would be to take away bereaved mothers and let us be together, and give us a chance to share our pain with people who can accept the pain, who can carry it, who aren't afraid of it. The idea of the workshop is not just a support group, but healing from all sides—spiritual, psychological, and physical. Shira and Shulamith and I plan two day workshops where we take fifteen bereaved women away and offer them massage, art therapy, narrative therapy, yoga and a chance to be away from their own families and take care of their own feelings. In June 2002, I manage to get funding for our first workshop for two days in a hotel in Hertzliya. I cry when I welcome the women to the seminar. It's an amazing feeling to be with women who are in the same situation. It is a feeling of being 'normal' with what is so abnormal.

The follow-up programs for the mothers are monthly meetings and Shira also calls the women each week to see how they're coping, to listen to whatever they have to say. We run more women's healing retreats. One woman at a retreat doesn't share her feelings at all, but at our next support group she speaks. She opens up. She tells the group that after losing two children in a terrorist attack, she felt that she couldn't go on; she felt so guilty, so bad, if she thought about one child, perhaps the other would be upset because she wasn't thinking about him. She was ready to kill herself, but then she realized that she had to accept God's decree, she had to take her suffering and live with it.

As I write this, we have already held six workshops for six different groups of women, together with follow-up programming for ninety women.

The women's healing workshop grows into family healing retreats where we take families away and provide opportunities for fun—hiking and rafting and jeeping for example, and healing groups where we work on expressing our feelings within the family. Many families don't normally talk about the child who is dead, don't discuss their pain. We work on opening up communication.

These projects are successful right away. Seth goes to the States each month to fundraise. I feel that these projects need to be born, that Israel is a society that has suffered from grief since its birth, and hasn't had the time or luxury to deal with pain. But it needs to. It is a hard society, where people are often abrasive and angry. Through the work of the Foundation, Koby has become a symbol of fun and healing, a symbol of love.

These projects help me. I need to take the love and support I've been given, the angels around me, and share them with the other mothers and families. I have been blessed with support and I bring that support to the other families. I feel that I am a channel for healing, an emissary, that my role is to give the other families what I've been given. It helps me to be with the other women and families. It helps us to see the children at the camp and the follow up reunion camps that we run three times during the year. It means that Koby's spirit is growing. Koby's capacity for joy, his great love, is in some way, staying alive.

Chapter forty-six
Gulls on the Beach

It's been ten months since Koby was killed. Grieving isn't really like labor because grieving doesn't end. I am left with the task of carrying Koby's dead body in my arms, taking it with me wherever I go. Bila Bachrach, whose eighteen-year-old son was murdered in Wadi Kelt in 1995, tells me that it is as if her son dies every day.

It is that way for me too. Each day, I have to work to go on; each day I decide to live. I am not the same person as I was. That is the way it should be. Losing Koby means that part of me was killed. But rather than mourn the person I was, I work to bless the person I have become.

The thought of a life without death scares me now. "Everlasting delight is no delight," say the Chassidic masters. And if death were to somehow be miraculously eradicated now, how would I ever be reunited with Koby?

The crystal from his grave sits over our dining room table. A crystal is a rock with a perfect pattern, a cell structure that repeats, obviously not random. In this rock, I read a message: There is a Maker, and he is fashioning me, carving my soul.

The crystal has six sides, like the Star of David, a structure that points to heaven and down below, connecting two worlds. Koby's death continues to create that connection for me. When the biblical Jacob slept at Beit El, the 'house of God,' with a stone at his head, he woke from his dream of angels of light ascending and descending a ladder and exclaimed: "How awesome is this place! This is none other than the dwelling of God!"

Grieving is also the place of God, a sacred space that connects heaven and earth. It is up to us as grievers to discover and dwell in that space.

I will never know or understand why Koby was killed, why he was murdered so brutally. But I think that his death has something to do with the history of this land, the ancient light hidden here, like the light in the olives in Tekoa, praised in the Talmud for their oil. The prophet Amos was a shepherd who lived in Tekoa, among the olive trees. Like an olive beaten for the light of its oil, "we shall be beaten and bruised, but in order to glow." (Chassidic Masters)

It is this olive oil that will anoint the Messiah—when we will be lamps radiating the light of God.

Nine months after Koby was killed, in Florida visiting my mother, I walked on the beach thinking I hadn't had any signs from Koby in a long time—no messages. In fact, in Florida I could hardly feel him. He was fading, becoming less distinct, less real to me. That hurt as much as missing him. Because I'd had had his voice inside of me for so long. And now I couldn't hear him.

I walked on the beach as the clouds skittered across the sun and I thought to myself: I need a sign from Koby. I need him. I need a message. When I returned to my spot, I took out my sandwich and bit into it. A gull swooped over me and hit me right in the head, knocking against me. Quickly I was surrounded by gulls that wanted my food.

Gulls are often hungry and greedy. But it was the first time in my life I had been hit by one, on the head.

My sister, Loren, said to me: "Koby's saying: 'What do I have to do, knock you over the head?'"

So the birds have flown to me to tell me that they have seen Koby.

Chapter forty-seven
The Bird's Nest

Birds, of all creatures, symbolize the connection between heaven and earth. We look at them and see the bliss of soaring between both worlds. They give us a taste of pure freedom. When God speaks to me, opening windows into the higher realms, those windows are opened for me by birds. The birds are my angels, telling me to look up and not sink into the gravity of my sadness.

I was looking for signs from God, but this one really took me by surprise. God took me in his arms and hugged me.

This bird story begins with a nest. Almost a year after Koby was killed, I dreamed that I was talking to God. I didn't see God, but I spoke to him. I said: "You say you are a God of compassion. Where is your compassion? How can you say you're a God of kindness after what you did to Koby?"

God answered me. "I am a God of compassion."

I answered. "How can you say that?"

God said, "I do the *mitzvah* of *shiluach ha ken*. The *mitzvah* of shooing away the mother bird."

In Deuteronomy, Chapter 22, verses 6 and 7, it is written: "If you happen upon a bird's nest before you on your way, in any tree or on the ground, with young ones or eggs, and the mother bird is sitting upon the young, or upon the eggs, do not take the mother with the young. You should send out the mother but the young you can take so that your days will be good and many."

Some say that this mitzvah teaches us compassion for animals, and by extension compassion for people. As I thought about my dream I realized that God had done me a kindness. I didn't witness Koby stolen from me, beaten, his head bloodied and pulverized. I did not have to see the actual physical destruction of my beloved son. But there are others who do. I met the mother of six-year-old Danielle Shefi who had seen her child murdered in her own home by a terrorist. So how can it be that the God who allows a mother to see her own child brutally murdered is one of compassion?

The Talmud has an answer for this unanswerable question. It says that whoever thinks that the *mitzvah* of shooing away the mother bird shows God's compassion should be silenced. Because they don't understand. We can't say that the *mitzvah* of shooing away the mother bird (I am later told, also a charm for fertility) is a symbol of God's compassion. Because we can't understand God's compassion. If the *mitzvah* were a true symbol of God's compassion, then surely we wouldn't be allowed to take the baby bird at all.

The morning following my dream, I went to a friend, a Torah teacher, to study with her. She said to me: "What do you want to study?" Before I could answer, she said: "I'm teaching the *mitzvah* of *shiluach ha ken* this week. Would you like to learn it?"

A coincidence? Or another sign from God? My friend and I learned that when the baby bird is taken, the mother returns to her nest and doesn't know where her babies have gone. She cries out because she has lost her children and lost her place in the world. It is that cry of loss and despair that awakens God's compassion into the world. As a result of that heartrending cry of loss, God comforts all those who have lost their place, who have troubles and pain and no place to rest.

As the mother bird cries, God lessens his harsh judgments on us and engages his mercy. It is our cry to God that urges God to increase his compassion and lead us toward redemption.

It seems like a cruel process. But in the next world, perhaps, we will accept this process as we see the way that our cries and pain led to the redemption of the world, a time and place of healing, love, and oneness with God.

The *mitzvah* of shooing away the mother bird is so important that one who performs the commandment of shooing her away receives great reward. It is one of the two commandments for which we receive long life in the Torah—the other one is respecting one's parents. Yet there is a story told in the Talmud of a boy whose father asks him to bring him bird's eggs. He climbs a ladder to get to the eggs, shoos away the mother bird, and falls from the ladder. He dies while performing the two commandments that are supposed to lead to long life. How can this be? It's beyond explanation, beyond our purview. Some say that 'a good life' means life in the next world. Some say that the point is quality not quantity. But how can our days be good here if our children are killed? Our children are our joy and our promise of long days, a kind of immortality in the world.

Perhaps achieving long days refers to the days of one's ancestors before you as well as your own days and your children's days. In other words, your days stretch forward and back—encompassing the continuity and quality of the previous generations. If you have taught your children to be respectful to you, to the world around them, and to God's word, then you have increased the days of those who have gone before you because they too experience pleasure in heaven as part of them observes the continuation of their goodness in this world.

I walked home from my studies, lost in thought. All I wanted was Koby. Before I walked into the house, I looked up. And there it was—suddenly a nest was hanging from a string from a rafter above the porch. It must have been there for a while since it was fully formed. It was right in front of my eyes, above the entrance of my home, and I had not seen it. I peered in; there were eggs nestled there.

So much is around us that we don't see, that we are not aware of. Koby must be near me, I thought. Near me, and yet I can't see him.

A few days later, I saw the mother bird darting about, a kind of hummingbird, plain, gray-brown, with a hooked beak. Occasionally, I glimpsed the father with brilliant blue-green spots of color under his wings.

About a week later, my children noticed baby birds in the nest and called me out to see them. As soon as we gathered by the nest, one bird fell out, onto the ground. My son Daniel put plastic gloves on and put him back in the nest. He was careful not to get his smell on the bird, so that the mother would not reject him.

It is said that in the cave, Rabbi Shimon Bar Yochai and his son studied with the prophet Elijah each day. One day, Rabbi Shimon and his son saw a hunter laying his snares for birds and spreading his traps. When the two mystics heard the voice of God whisper: "Pardon them," the bird went free. But when they heard the voice whisper: "His time's up!" the bird was trapped and taken.

Rabbi Shimon said: "There is Providence even in the fall of a sparrow. If this is true of a bird, how such more so of a human being."

They decided to leave the cave and return to the world.

Outside our porch, the baby birds survived.

At the one-year anniversary of Koby's death, the *yahrzeit*, during the eulogies at the cemetery, a lone bird soared overhead, squawking as though he were calling to us. Many people remarked on it, most of whom knew nothing of my newfound connection to birds. We returned to the house that day for classes and lunch and a community hike through the canyon where Koby was murdered. As a group of women sat in my front yard learning about the meaning of the World-to-Come, the baby birds from our nest fluttered in and out. All week they tested their wings, flapping back and forth to the nest. And then a week later, the birds flew away. The nest was no longer needed, the whole family was gone.

A gift to me. A gift of beauty and a taste of freedom.

A week after Koby's *yahrzeit*, at my son Daniel's *Bar Mitzvah*, birds also made an appearance. It was difficult for all of us to celebrate the *Bar Mitzvah*, but it was a relief to open our hearts to happiness. Nancy, a distant cousin whom I hadn't seen since Koby's *shiva* week brought a small gift box to the party. Her brother had died thirty years earlier, a young teenager killed in a horseback riding accident. Nancy was eleven when her brother died.

"Come see what I've brought you," she said. And when she lifted the lid, I was stunned when I saw what she had inside. Baby birds. They had fallen out of a nest and friends had brought them to her to keep alive. She was feeding them with a dropper and had to keep them with her, under her watchful care.

I'd never told her the way birds recently kept appearing in my life.

Another sign from God.

King David himself understood the power of birds. There is no creature whose voice resonates more powerfully with ours. Once King David awakened from his dreams and began to compose his heavenly songs, the Psalms, dedicated to the Temple, the dwelling of God on this earth. With his power of prophecy David foresaw that the Temple would be destroyed. He worried about what would happen to the heavenly music he had composed. When he looked around for a custodian of the beautiful sound, he realized that he could vouchsafe his song to the birds.

It is said that on the day the enemy chased the Jews away from the Temple, the birds also flew away. But they kept the song of the Temple alive. Perhaps that was the song my husband and I heard the night of the funeral, the night that sound turned to touch.

One day the birds will return the song to the temple.

And that return will be sparked by holy events occurring in another bird's nest—a mystical nest in the heavens. According to the *Zohar*, there are birds' nests not just in this world, but in the upper worlds. In the Garden of Eden of the upper world is a bird's nest. It is the most secret, most hidden place of the world. On the walls are pictures of our enemies and pictures of the holy Temple. And in that bird's nest the Messiah waits. In the nest are pictures of all of the Jewish children who have died sanctifying God's name.

The Messiah goes in and out and in and out of the nest, waiting to redeem the world, waiting for a pillar of light to form between this world and the next, signifying that it is time for him to enact justice in the world. He waits with the souls of the children who died sanctifying God's name, children like Koby and Yosef who died for being Jews. Their pictures are there. What are the pictures? They are the memories of the mothers who will never forget, who will never let their children die because they live on inside of them.

Perhaps the bird's nest is telling us that nothing is ever really lost, not a piece of wood, not a feather, not a stray bit of string, nor our murdered children. We are all part of some grand design, some grand purpose. We are all under God's watchful care. Our job is to enhance the holiness of the world, no matter how many babies are stolen from the nest. God tells us he will not forget. Neither will we. But we will keep building, keep creating places of love and rest and sanctity; keep nurturing our families with warmth and love and strength. We will keep reminding ourselves: the world is a mystery, but God is with us, like a nest that protects us. One day, the Messiah will fly forth from the supernal bird's nest and bring healing to the world. We will understand how Elijah and Shimon Bar Yochai and Koby and all of the murdered children have forged that redemption. We will sing like birds as we are reunited with our children. We will understand the blessing of a broken heart. Once again, I will stand with Koby, and he will tell me that all those hugs from God were hugs from him as well.

Memorial plaque at the site of the murder.

The inscription reads:
"With your powerful arm, you redeemed your people, the sons of Jacob and Joseph."
Here in this place, on the earth of this good land, our beloved, sweet children were
murdered by savages. In their lives and their deaths they were not parted.
Yaakov Natan Mandell – Yosef Ish-Ran
May God avenge their deaths
15th Iyyar, 5761
8th May 2001
"Their graceful faces, the fruits of our wombs, our sons, how have they fallen?"

Chapter forty-eight
A Year On

It is Koby and Yosef's *yahrzeit*. About five hundred of us march through the wadi, some carrying flags, a ribbon of young people and old people, climbing the rugged paths. Wild mustard, garlic, irises, anemones dot the steep slopes. I have not been to the wadi since Koby was killed. I do not know if I will enter the cave. It is too painful for me, the thought of the last hours of Koby's life, the struggle to fight for life, his dying alone. But suddenly we are in the cleft of the rock; there is an opening in the stone to stoop under. The cave has been cleaned of the boys' blood. There is the sound of the wind instead of the cry of screams. When I enter the cave it is full of candles, the light seems to magnify and expand, so that I am in a place of beauty and wonder. A large cone-shaped pile of rocks is on the side of the cave. My husband tells me that under these rocks are the blood stained rocks that were used to kill Koby and Yosef. According to religious law, these bloodstained rocks have been buried by the *chevra kadisha*, the Jewish burial society. All of the blood has returned to the earth.

My husband turns to me: "This cave now feels holy."

This year I have learned that everything, even the worst trial, contains sparks of holiness and it is up to us to release those sparks and bring them into the world.

Even the bad, in Jewish thought, deserves blessing. "Just as one utters blessing over the bad, so should he utter blessing over the good," (*Berachot*, 54a).

I do not bless the bad. But I understand that light comes from darkness, and that evil exists in the world so that we can choose to do good. Evil exists to be conquered. As the Talmud says: If nothing but good existed it would be like carrying a lamp in broad daylight. It would provide no benefit. Ultimately everything is for the good, even when we can't see it.

God does his work with that which is broken. We humans can only use vessels if they are unbroken: we can't put a broken pail into the well and drink. Yet it is when our hearts are broken that God sculpts our souls, prodding open the narrow entrances to the caves of our being. Whenever God takes from you, he has to give you something back. God has given me the blessing of a broken heart.

I feel as if I am moving out of the darkness of the cave. God is carrying my family and me on his outspread wings, to a nest where—though we feel exposed and vulnerable—we will be able to celebrate the beauty of nature and the wonder of the world.

A nest is a place of light and protection, a place that enables flight. If the cave is the place of the prophets, the bird's nest is the place of the Messiah, a place that surrounds, but leaves one free. It is not a place of struggle, but a place where one is nurtured, fed, loved. The darkness of the cave is always there waiting for me. But so is the freedom of the bird's nest, the vision of being protected yet vulnerable, safe yet exposed to the elements—open to the air, to the night, to the cold. It is not a place that swallows you, like the cave, but a place that opens you so that you have a fuller encounter with the world. It is not easy to reach the birds' nest, to believe in the bird's nest. But sometimes now I dwell in the bird's nest, and sense that it is God who is hovering over me, protecting me.

It is there, in the nest, that we sense our love for each other, for Koby, and for God. It is from this place that we truly and most vibrantly sing out our praise like the birds in the early morning, celebrating the birth of a new day.

Chapter forty-nine

Koby's Articles

(written for *wholefamily.com*)

Taking the Bully by the Horns:
A Review of Kathy Noll's Nasty People

By Koby Mandell

I was once bullied by a jerk who wanted to show off in front of his friends. He took a chair from me during school when I was sitting down and I fell on the floor. I said to my friends that guy's an idiot and he heard me. He started to hit and kick me and then walked away. I didn't hit him back because he was bigger and older than me. A week later my father found out and we ran into him at the pizza place. My father went up to him and threatened to break his nose off if he touched me again. Since then he has not bothered me. I felt good because he was punished and embarrassed.

The book, *Nasty People*, explains why bullies bully. Now I understand that he bothered me because he felt really small inside and I was an easy target because I was new in the school. People used to make fun of him because of his grades and he probably felt bad about himself and decided to take it out on other people.

I liked this book because it tells you how to take care of bullies, why they are bullies and what makes a bully. It tells about the bully cycle: when somebody gets bullied after a while he tries to act tough and bullies when he is feeling very small inside and lacks respect for his self. It's a good book and it teaches you how to take care of bullies. You confront him with the problem and then he'll understand that he's doing something wrong, and try to reform. If he doesn't, just ignore him.

A bully picks somebody so that he can take his anger about feeling bad about himself out on somebody else. He picks somebody smaller than him without too many friends. Somebody he thinks won't tell anybody.

In my class kids are still bullying other kids but I'm not getting bullied because they know if they bother me, I'll beat them up. If I see somebody bullying I try to stop him. When a big person is pushing a little person in line to go to the water fountain, I tell him to stop, for example.

It also tells how to know if you're a victim or not. If you feel bad and you don't know why, if you have dreams that you're a Ninja fighter, if you dream of revenge, if you avoid passing people's houses, then you're a victim.

You've got to confront the bully.

If he ignores you, then you've got to get help from an adult.

What Makes a Good Parent

By Koby Mandell, Age 13

If I were my parents, I would always stick up for my kid because if you don't, your kid begins to feel bad and thinks that you don't care about him. Anyway, your kid always needs somebody to stick up for him.

I would also let my kid wear whatever he wants and make his own decisions, because kids need freedom as much as parents do, if not more.

I'm not saying you can let your kid do whatever he wants, but don't confine him, and let him make his own decisions.

I would also let him keep his room however he wants. But tell him to clean it once a week. If he doesn't want to clean it, don't make him—just close the door. Make sure that nobody cleans up for him.

Let him pick his own friends. If you don't like one of his friends, then tell him that. If he doesn't want to change his friends, tell him that you won't let the friend come in the house. But still don't take him away from his friends unless he's doing something really bad like drugs.

Go out of your way for him but don't change your course. Which means you can go out of your way for him but don't cancel something important for yourself for something not so important for him. Like going to the mall or going to a friend's house.

Let him do what he wants, work with what he wants, and how he wants to work. Let him take as much time as he can. But that doesn't mean he can wait a week if you need something done now. Like bringing down the laundry or taking out the garbage.

School: Make a schedule together of when he's going to do his homework and projects, when and what he is going to do for after-school activities, and when he is going to eat dinner each day. And make sure to ask if he has homework and if he doesn't, ask him what subjects he had today and what he had to do in each one. That way he'll 'remember' the homework better.

Have meetings with his teacher every other month to check how he's doing. If he's not doing that well, talk to him about it but be gentle. Sometimes he's doing as good as he can.

Dinner: Dinner is one of the most important meals that you should have together at the same time always with a full meal, including drinks, salad, and a main course. And when the kids are good—dessert. During dinner, you should ask the kids how their day was, what they did, and what happened. After dinner, you do not have to serve any more dinners, but you can serve snacks. After 9:30 P.M., the kitchen should close for you. Your kids can still go in and get whatever they want.

Chores: Everybody should get their share of chores and the parents should also do their share of chores. If the kids do their chores right for a week, give them a little prize or take them out for dinner.

Allowances: Kids should get allowances according to their age. Like you don't give a five-year-old a buck. But you do give an eight-year-old a buck. For every year, the kids' allowance should go up by at least a half a dollar. Start giving allowance (about a quarter) at the age of five. So kids can learn the value of a dollar. But they have to do chores for the money.

How to talk to your kids: Talk to your kids gently. And not that much. Let the kids do the talking. If they need encouragement to talk, start talking a lot and then let them pick up. At the end the parents should do almost no talking and just say, uh huh, and yes.

How I think my mother is doing: My mother is doing okay, but I don't think she gives me enough allowance and we don't have dinner together or a schedule of homework.

All in all, she's OK, though. If she reads this article, maybe she'll do a bit better.

226

Appendix
About the Foundation

C AMP KOBY AND YOSEF is a camp for some four hundred bereaved children and orphans, whose parents or siblings have been killed by terrorists. The camp is a combination of fun and healing, with camps during the summer and school holidays and a 'Big Brother—Big Sister' follow up program.

The WOMEN'S HEALING RETREATS enable groups of widows and bereaved mothers to attend two-day workshops in a hotel away from home—so as to give them a real break. The Retreats nurture women physically, psychologically and spiritually, with sessions that include narrative therapy, group counseling, massage and yoga. Follow up programming includes individual weekly phone counseling by a grief counselor and monthly meetings with the group.

In the FAMILY HEALING RETREATS, families struck by terror are able to get away for a three-day vacation that combines fun activities like jeeping, hiking and kayaking with separate healing groups for children, teens, mothers and fathers. The goal is to enhance communication within the families.

YOUNG ADULT HEALING RETREATS, for adults between twenty

and thirty, provide fun, healing experiences where young adults can share and cope with the special problems they face in being part of bereaved families.

THE KOBY MANDELL FOUNDATION
To learn more about the Koby Mandell Foundation
and our healing programs,

please email us:
info@kobymandell.org
Visit our website http://www.kobymandell.org

write or call us:
c/o Todd Sukol
Sukol Communications
7272 Wisconsin Ave. Suite 300
Bethesda, Maryland 20814
301 654 8868 (within the U.S.)

or:
Seth and Sherri Mandell
Box 97
Tekoa, Israel 90908
smandell@actcom.co.il

Bibliography

Amichai, Yehuda, *Great Tranquility: Questions and Answers*, Harper and Row: New York, 1983.

Ariel, David, *The Mystic Quest*, Schocken Books: New York, 1988.

Baifus, Rabbi Yaakov Yisrael, *Longing for Dawn* (translated by Rabbi Nachman Bulman), Feldheim Publishers: Nanuet, New York, 1995.

Belsky, Judy, *A Thread of Blue*, Targum Press: 1992 (out of print)

Buber, Martin, *Ten Rungs: Hasidic Sayings*, Schocken Books: New York, 1947.

———, *Tales of the Hasidim: Early Masters*, Schocken Books: New York, 1975.

———, *The Legend of the Baal-Shem*, Schocken Books: New York, 1955.

Goldberg, Rabbi Chaim Binyamin, *Mourning in Halacha* (translated by Shlomo Fox-Ashrei), Mesorah Publishers: New York, 1991.

Gottlieb, Freema, *The Lamp of God*, Jason Aronson: New Jersey, 1989.

Hoffman, Edward, *The Heavenly Ladder*, Harper and Row: San Francisco, 1985.

Kahana, Dr. S.Z. Israel, *Legends*, Machbarot Lesifrut Publishers: Israel, 1969.

Kaplan, Aryeh, *Made in Heaven*, Moznaim Publishing Corp.: Brooklyn, 1983.

Klapholtz, Yisroel Yaakov, *Stories of Elijah the Prophet*, Pe'er Hasefer Publishers: Bnei Beraq, 1978.

Lamm, Maurice, *The Jewish Way in Death and Mourning*, Jonathan David Publishers: New York, 1969.

Langer, Jiri, *Nine Gates to the Chassidic Mysteries*, McKay: New York, 1961.

Lewis, C.S., *A Grief Observed*, Bantam: New York, 1961.

Moffat, Mary Jane, editor, *In the Midst of Winter: Selections from the Literature of Mourning*, Vintage: *New York*, 1982.

Remen, Rachel Naomi, *Kitchen Table Wisdom*, Riverhead Books: New York, 1997.

———, *My Grandfather's Blessings*, Riverhead Books: New York, 2001.

Shapira, Rabbi Kalonymous Kalmish, *Sacred Fire* (translated by J. Hershy Worch), Jason Aronson: New Jersey, 2000.

Sittser, Gerald, *A Grace Disguised: How the Soul Grows Through Loss*, Zondervan Publishing House: Michigan, 1995.

Tucazinsky, Rabbi N.A., *Gesher Hachaim: The Bridge of Life*, Moznaim Publishing Corporation: New York, 1983.

Wiesel, Elie, *Sages and Dreamers*, Summit Books: New York, 1991.

Wolpe, Rabbi David, *Making Loss Matter*, Riverhead Books: New York, 1999.

Zornberg, Dr Avivah Gottlieb, *The Particulars of Rapture*, Doubleday: New York, 2001.

———, *Genesis: The Beginning of Desire*, Doubleday: New York, 1995.

Acknowledgments

To my husband—your love is my comfort. To my children, Daniel, Eliana and Gavi, for their joyful spirits and resilient hearts; To Rena and Ezra Ish-Ran, sister and brother in loss.

To my family—my parents, Paul Lederman (of blessed memory) and Marilyn Lederman, who taught me to appreciate joy and to know that life is full of the unexpected; to my sister, Nancy Lederman, for joining us at the *shiva* so that I could laugh as well as cry, and to my sister and brother-in-law Richie and Loren Fogelson for their love, car, and trips to the airport. And to my Mandell family—Marcy, Larry, Marilyn, and Richard, for always making me feel at home; and especially to my mother-in-law, Lillian Mandell, for being one of my greatest fans and for sharing tears with me.

To Shira Chernoble, healer and wise woman; to Valerie Seidner, for daily love and kindness; to Anne Breslow for her depth of understanding and the trip to the beach; to Shulamith Lando, who taught me about waking dreams and helped me release the trauma; to Andrea Peskoff for her sensitivity, intelligence, and calls; to Ruth Mason and Bob Trachtenberg for the careful attention and special favors; to Chantal Danino Holt for love, encouragement, and birthday celebrations; to Esther Wolfson, for her phone calls and thoughtful contributions; to Shari Rosenfeld for making sure we were taken care of. To Fran Ackerman who stayed with me through the worst pain.

To my neighbors who came close and stay there…I can't name you all. Hadara Reisinger, Ruthi Wallfish, Linda Brown, Judy Lowe, Leah Birnbaum, Rochelle Templeman, Beverly Ungar, Dana Millstein, Michelle Bieber and Barbara Sutnik nurtured me; Aviva Sutnik stayed with me during those most vulnerable nights; Tanya painted and redecorated. Jerry Freund keeps me in reading and organic broccoli; Ruchie Kohlenberg made sure I returned from vacation to a clean house. To Shimon Seidner for his deep feelings and his fried chicken; to Eli Birnbaum, for his history lessons; to Yossi Templeman for his printer help; Michael Pomerantz for his books on Elijah; to Arieh Breslow for teaching me Tai Chi; to Steve Peskoff for his Spanish conversations; to Steve and Debbie Feuerstein, new friends who gave us a tour of Hong Kong and media coaching; to Avraham and Shoshana HaCohen for their help and reassuring presence; and to the group of women from Efrat who anonymously sent me Sabbath meals for six months.

And more thanks to Yael Solomon, Todd and Amy Sukol, Reni Isser, Linda Zurndorfer, Debbie and Art Sapper, Tuvia and Faigy Grauman, Rochelle Edelson, Ginny Twersky, Limor Hershkovitz, and Debbie Nodiff. Great thanks to Alan and Rachel Silverman for their hospitality at Camp Moshava. To Koby's hero, Cal Ripken, who read our story in the *Baltimore Jewish Times* and contacted us because he wants to be involved, wants to build a baseball stadium in Israel in Koby's honor.

A special thank you to my teachers—Michal Shir El, for singing with me on the Sabbath; Malka Petrokovsy, for her teaching and *Shabbat* visits; to Hadassah Froman who shared her warmth and wisdom; Yardena Yosef for her teachings; Mira Cohen, who shared her love of the Psalms with me; and a special thank you to Diane Liff, who taught me that learning can mean one foot leaving the ground. I am indebted to Sara Schneider, whose knowledge of Jewish mysticism illuminated some of the mysteries in my loss, and I thank Avivah Gottlieb Zornberg, whose lectures helped me conceptualize the arc of this book. I am grateful to Sara Eisen for her careful corrections and editing help on the manuscript and to Rabbi Avi Wallfish for his helpful editing comments.

My thanks to Matthew Miller and the staff at the Toby Press for their sensitivity and appreciation. A special thank you to my agent Deborah Harris who found the right nest for this book and to Aloma Halter, my editor, who responded to this book with love and intelligence.

To the staff of the Koby Mandell Foundation for your fantastic caring work—especially Reuven Angstreich—and to the staff and to all of the mothers at our Mothers' Healing Retreats. To all of you who have contributed to the Koby Mandell Foundation—my thanks for blessing my family with the fullness of your hearts.